R^{The}esilient

Parent

Everyday Wisdom for Life with your Exceptional Child

R^{The}esilient
Parent

Everyday Wisdom for Life with your Exceptional Child

by: Mantu Joshi

649

Pittsboro, NC
drt press   www.drtpress.com

Published by DRT Press, P.O. Box 427, Pittsboro, NC 27312, www.drtpress.com. Copyright © 2013 DRT Pres s. All rights reserved. No part of this publication may be reproduced or transmitted in any form or by any means, electronic or mechanical, including photocopy or any information storage and retrieval system without permission from the copyright holder and publisher. To inquire about quantity discount please contact the publisher.

Book design by www.duckofalltrades.com
Additional cover design help by Ritu Parr.

"I'm not perfect," © Laurie Berkner Band. Used with permission.

Publisher's Cataloging-in-Publication data

Joshi, Manohar.
    The Resilient parent : everyday wisdom for life with an exceptional child / by Mantu Joshi.
        p. cm.
        ISBN 978-1-933-084251 (pbk.)
        ISBN 978-1-933-084268 (e-book)
        ISBN 978-1-933-084275 (Kindle)
1. Parents of children with disabilities. 2. Children with disabilities. 3. Resilience (Personality trait). 4. Self realization. 5. Self actualization (Psychology). 6. Child rearing. 7. Parenting. I. Title.

HQ759.913 .J67 2014
649.152 --dc23   2013954239

Table of Contents

A note from the author

This book would not have been possible without the support and care of key people in my family's life. First and foremost, Joy. She is my spouse, my sanity, my lover, my best friend, and my parenting partner. She was the first to encourage me to write. She was my first reader and gave me key critical feedback at the very beginning.

I also want to thank Kelly Jeske, a friend who inspired and encouraged my writing efforts. She was instrumental in connecting me with DRT Press. Lisa Porter from *Sensory Kids*, a center in Portland that helps kids with SPD (Sensory Processing Disorder), was an early reader and also helped me in getting the word out about the book.

I cannot say enough about Adrienne Ehlert Bashista from DRT Press. She believed in the importance of this project to support parents. She coached, prodded, and midwifed this work in ways that most writers would only dream of from a publisher. Along those lines, Karen Pullen's editing really made this book accessible, and its clarity is largely owed to her careful hand. I also sincerely appreciate the work of rest of the DRT Press team:

Erin Baldwin, copyeditor, and Jeff Duckworth, designer.

I want to thank my team of caregivers that gave me those key few hours of respite to be more mindful in my parenting. Molly Smartt, Jenna Cohan, Megan Daline, and Vicky and Michael Axthelm (extraordinary grandparents), all came in at various times and enriched our children's lives while I hammered out a few more pages.

I want to thank my parents, Avinash and Pratibha Joshi for their patience with my special needs as a kid, and for modeling taking care of a child's self-esteem.

My cousin Tara Masih was wise counsel in navigating the publishing world.

Most of all, I want to thank Nicole and Michael (and Joy Junior too!) for being such exceptional children. I am so proud of the people they are becoming and the resilience they show every day.

Thanks,
Mantu

Introduction

Many of us parents are dealing with a challenge that was not necessarily of our choosing. If you feel hurt, confused, angry, depressed, or worried about raising a child with special needs, you are not alone. Your feelings are legitimate and need room to breathe.

Yet, in the midst of the hurt and confusion, beyond the pain and maybe some shame, is real hope. Not the greeting card kind of hope, nor the kind that comes from denial. No. I am talking about a deeper hope that is about finding your best self as you live through the challenges of your everyday demands.

If you feel stressed out and overwhelmed, and want to feel more grounded in your parenting, the ideas in this book are for you. When burnout isn't an option, you need to take care of yourself. I am not talking about massages or vacations, although those are great! Some of us don't have the time or support to get away, and we probably can't afford a massage or two every week. We need to care for ourselves in the middle of the struggle. We need to have options that are life-giving for both ourselves and our child in everyday life.

This book is written by a parent in the trenches who knows what it is to live at the intersection of bone-tired and dispirited. In this book, I have shared with you some of the insights and precious gifts I have received from being with my two children with special needs. Their strength and resilience has taught me so much and has deepened my perspective.

You might feel like much of your life is closing up, but I want to tell you that it may be that your whole life is about to open in ways you could not have imagined before. If you are mindful of what you are doing and why you are doing it, you can reframe the picture in your head so that your life stands out in new ways. This book is about moving from a place of struggle with parenting a child with special needs, to a place of life, health, and deeper meaning.

Some people seem to have remarkable self-knowledge, impeccable parenting instincts, and inner strength. They navigate peaceably through any difficulty. This book is for the rest of us, who, with clenched teeth, an exhausted body, and a pounding headache, need reminders to keep centered and balanced along the journey.

From the outside, our family seems like a candidate for some kind of crazed reality show. I will introduce my family, using their middle names to protect their privacy.

My wife, Joy, is a brilliant psychologist, caring mother, and the primary breadwinner of the family. She is blind and uses a guide dog.

Our oldest child, Nicole, is six. She struggles with sensory issues and has ADHD with a leaning toward Oppositional Defiant Disorder. She can bolt at a minute's notice and has been known to lie down in the street with her eyes closed just to drive us crazy.

Our son, Michael, age five, is on the edge of being diagnosed with Reactive Attachment Disorder and has issues with his temper. He has nearly broken both of our noses and has left us black and blue many times. He has also been delayed developmentally and has learning challenges.

Both of our older kiddos were adopted out of foster care, and their special needs may stem from their complex birth histories. We adopted out of foster care because we believe deeply that all children deserve loving, permanent, and safe homes. We particularly felt drawn to adopting right out of our own community.

After this book was written, we had a third child, Joy Jr., and she is a typical child as far as we can tell. She is now six months old.

I have been in ministry for about twenty years and a stay-at-home dad for the last five years. I have also had some training as an interfaith chaplain, and I have done some advanced studies in worship rituals.

I have been diagnosed with ADD of the inattentive type. So, all of us have special needs in our family, with the exception of our new baby.

I have shared our challenges, but I would be remiss in not sharing some of our strengths as well. Joy is the most tenacious person I know and may be the first blind person to be on faculty at a medical school. Nicole is the most generous child I have ever met. She is smart. With play breaks, visual reminders, and other extra help, she caught up two years of school in one year. Michael is a gifted musician and can tap out any rhythm on demand. He also claims to be the second fastest kid on the playground at his preschool. Our baby girl has slept through the night at least once!

This book describes our journey as we learned to cope with our different ways of being in the world. It is my gift to other parents and caregivers who feel like their families could use some relief.

It is also a locker room pep talk to give the strength you will need to remain resilient, despite your exhaustion in overtime.

You will notice that I use different faith perspectives from time to time. My knowledge of these faiths comes largely from ecumenical work as a pastor and my early training in interfaith chaplaincy. My training was at the ultradiverse Alta-Bates Summit Medical Center, very close to the UC-Berkley campus in Berkley, California.

Although an ordained United Methodist minister, I was expected to support people of all faiths in crisis. There was no intent to cover all faiths in this book; these ideas flowed naturally out of my own reflection while parenting. Even if you do not have an identified faith, you might find you can benefit as well from each tradition's wisdom.

Each section has reflection questions, which are really at the heart of finding your resilience. You can ruminate on these on your own or share them in your circle of support.

Read this book in any order you choose. Read it from cover to cover, or just open it and read whatever presents itself to you. You may have only a minute between pickups or drop-offs, or just before bed. This book was written for those in the midst of the struggle, so abandon all the rules and just enjoy it, knowing that it was written for you and your self-care as a parent. It is my hope that you will discover the resilient parent you already are.

Write A New Job Description: The Family Joy Maker

Somehow, I felt like a slave in my own home. The physical demands of taking care of the kids was beginning to make homemaking an endless set of chores. Even the fun things that we did were aimed toward burning up the kids' energy. Usually my own energy disappeared first. Honestly, after two years of being a stay-at-home Dad, I was tired of being a homemaker.

I did not stay at home because I loved making a home. I was home because my wife and I had decided it made more sense for me to be Nicole's primary caretaker. After our family grew with Michael, and we discovered slowly that he had even more needs and emotional instability, we decided it would be better for me to continue to be the one anchoring home duty. My spouse also earned more income than I and could support all the needed therapies and expenses.

One day I was particularly dispirited by the chaos of our home. The dishes from the day before were precariously piled in the sink so high that there was no longer room for the breakfast dishes. All three hampers were overflowing, and our bed was so cluttered with mail that the cat was yowling that he could not find a place to curl up. The kids had just trashed the playroom, and I had a hard time finding enough counter space to make up lunches for the kids. As I was pulling another load of laundry out of the dryer, I had an insight about my work, an awakening of spirit! The truth was that I was not a homemaker at all—or rather, I did not understand what homemaking was really about.

My jo b was to create a place, a space, and an attitude that produced joy. A homemaker was actually a joy maker. A clean home and folded clothes were not items to be crossed off my list but steps toward my goal—to produce joy.

This sounds simple, but how many of us do things for our spouses or our kids and then resent it when no one appreciates the work? Yet things shift when we are not working to get people to appreciate us. We are making joy happen.

Sometimes creating joy is messy. One late afternoon I was making soup for the kids. Normally, I would have put on a video for the kids while I got the food ready as fast as possible. Instead, realizing that I was making joy, not just soup, I took out two extra bowls. I gave them all the food scraps as we went along, and they pretended to make soup. The result was a lot of joy and a little more mess—

actually, a lot more mess—but in the end they ate the healthy soup, and we followed our meal with one of those moments you never think you are going to have anymore with all the special-needs drama. We danced and celebrated our bliss, made even sweeter by the fact that I knew that this kind of joy was what we needed to survive another day. Creating joy is the secret recipe ingredient for the resilient parent.

● ● ● ● ● ● ● ●

How does going from home-making to joy-making shift your thinking? What does a joyful household look like to you? What is one chore you want to approach differently with the goal of producing joy?

I am the family-health coordinator

I had a membership to a health club, but my son Michael's special needs kept getting him kicked out of the gym's childcare. Apparently they did not like it when he responded to a request to share his matchbox car with a knuckle sandwich across the caregiver's nose. I had to quit the health club and gave up on exercise.

But as I began to shift my thinking, I realized that I could not wait for the kids to get better for me to be healthy. I got out the jogging stroller, despite my embarrassment that half the canopy hung off to the side, and started jogging to pick up Nicole from preschool. It was only a ten-minute run. Now, a ten-minute workout three times a week is pathetic for a lot of people, but I decided that I was the health coordinator and I would change things as needed, no other voices allowed in my head! I took the kids to the backyard for an hour every day, and I started to stick little sprints and exercises into our day.

Slowly, my kids started to follow my example. The other day, Michael, who never moves unless forced, jumped up and ran to one of his therapy appointments. I had to walk fast to keep up with my formerly sedentary child.

I am the family-health coordinator and can encourage exercise however I see fit.

• • • • • • • •

Where can you "see fit" in your daily routine right now? Are there places you could walk instead of ride? Can you stretch while waiting, or do ten sit-ups while playing with the kids?

I am the Zen coordinator

Michael cannot adapt quickly to changes in his routine. He is rigid in his desires. One day, his sister, Nicole, woke him up, instead of me. She wanted to let him know there was a special breakfast for him downstairs. He pulled down his pants in anger and urinated all over her.

On previous occasions, I have to admit that, being human and fed up, I'd yell out my frustration. He'd quiet down, so my reaction seemed to work. But a day later, he would just repeat whatever I had said the day before, only much louder, more angrily.

As a management strategy, yelling backfired. Furthermore, I found that my spirit was depleted whenever I responded angrily. I finally realized that to protect my spirit, I needed to practice patience. I focused less on shaping him and more on myself.

It took practice. Just like playing scales on the piano is a practiced art, I began to teach myself not to react as much. Practicing was not easy, especially at first. I had to force myself to breathe at times, but my role in the family was to demonstrate some Zen.

When Michael urinated all over his sister, I remembered my Zen and calmly walked him through cleaning up his sister and the floor. It took us four hours to get through it, but I kept my calm, and he has not tried that particular strategy since.

· · · · · · · ·

What are the times you feel most calm? What normally invites that stillness into your being? Is it a piece of music, a cup of coffee, a deep breath, or walking bare foot in the grass? Can you find opportunities to do those little things during your day? If being calm is a practiced art, at what point in your daily routine do you need to practice calm the most?

Surrender a spotless home

Nicole is a master of disaster when it comes to creating instant messes in our home.

We were trying to sell our house. I wanted to keep it picked up, clean, and ready to show at all times, so I was constantly watching over her, thwarting her active play, and anticipating destruction. It was exhausting for both of us.

What I began to realize was that most of the time the damage was minimal and that my reaction was draining my spirit, a worse consequence than the damage to the home.

For instance, my Nicole decided that her very oily hair spray was glass cleaner and squirted it all over the bathroom mirror. I was about to explode when I realized that of course, to her, this was just her way of helping me with my chores. I needed to be a little more Zen about it. As it turned out, the mirror was not nearly as hard to clean as I feared. By the time I had cleaned the bathroom, I was calmer, ready to clean up whatever she had exploded in the rest of the house.

• • • • • • • • •

Do you overreact to the messes your kids make? Does it feel like they instantly undo every effort of yours to keep our home under control? Does it feel personal? How can you be more Zen about it and see things through your child's eyes? What would letting go of the fantasy of a spotless home mean for your sanity?

I am my own relief pitcher, so what needs to change?

I have to admit: as the stay-at-home parent, I began to shut down around 5 p.m. I was ready for the working spouse to get home and give me some help. I wanted someone to take over! I was tired, like the sore starting pitcher who wants a break. We didn't live near our family, and we were new to our neighborhood, so relief was not going to happen. Still, what was my attitude doing to my spouse's spirit and to our relationship? I needed to share the work, but simply handing off the kids made me bitter and did not foster a sense of family. This was not like baseball, where the manager could replace me and I could trot to the dugout for a rest.

I needed a better model. The learning happened while my spouse was gone for a week and I was my own relief pitcher. I'd been spending my evenings zoned out in front of the TV, going to bed later, then feeling tired and drained the next day. Realizing the price of so much tube time, I made a radical change: I unplugged the TV and symbolically moved it to the basement. What was I thinking? I had just removed my baby sitter, my relief pitcher. My kids were going to go crazy. I would never get anything done!

To my surprise, the kids took it well. I rearranged the TV room to create more open play space. During their former TV time (around 3:30 or so) I sat down with them and read books. They were so well settled that I let them continue to play while I made dinner. After I put them to bed, I found I was not as tired. I set things up for the next morning and went to bed. What a difference an extra hour of sleep made. At the end of the day, I had energy, and I did not waste it. Bit by bit, every day, I got a little more organized and less frazzled.

● ● ● ● ● ● ● ●

What would happen if you gave your TV or game box a vacation? What if you took a month off every season from media? What would need to change to make that happen?

"Not enough time" is less accurate than "not enough energy"

The big lie we tell ourselves is that we do not have enough time. If single parent J.K. Rowling could write a children's book and Potterrize the world, then we have enough time. I know, I know. If you have kids with special needs, the whole world seems to be caving in all around, and you really do have less time. But when I would get to evening and crash every day, and as that pattern got worse, I realized a more accurate truth: time *was* available. It was energy that was escaping me.

Getting moving at the beginning of the day, overcoming inertia, was a real energy depleter. For instance, because the laundry had not been folded the night before, my whole morning was chaotic as I tried to find matched socks and underwear for everyone. Digging through the pile of dishes left over from a late night to find spoons for cereal was draining.

I came to realize that my flagging energy was the problem, not lack of time.

How could I generate and sustain energy? Rather than grab an energy drink, which tended to make me more irritable in the long run, I needed a better system.

I decided to get clothes and food ready for the morning the night before. No easy task—I was so depleted from helping the kids get to bed that most nights I would just veg in front of the TV or read my email. Each night I would tell myself I could do the work in the morning. But the reality is that multitasking with kids with special needs is never easy and takes a lot more energy. Energy while the kids are sleeping is invaluable. What can you do at night that will give you momentum in the morning? You will save yourself a lot stress, and you will actually add energy to your day even before you begin it.

Another big energy drain on us parents is worrying. Whenever the school calls about a new behavioral problem or the kids are in a regression pattern, we can get into problem-solving mode. When this is constructive, it's a healthy coping mechanism. Most of the time, however, we use the worry to perseverate on our own lack of control. We might fire off a half-dozen emails or sit on the couch and stew. Don't waste your energy!

When I began to think about my energy being finite, I realized that the worry needed to be compartmentalized. I began to save my worry for later. I decided I would be positive until I made it to another monthly support group meeting, and then I would let the anxiety have its due. Until then, I would not waste the energy.

Amazingly, these two changes—preparing for the day the night before and compartmentalizing worry—completely changed my energy reserve. I found myself laughing and joking more often. My seemingly endless fatigue began to lift, and I began to be full of life again.

When I became more mindful of not only my time but also my energy, things began to fall into place.

• • • • • • • • •

What is one thing you can prepare for the morning routine?

What is one person or group that you can put on the calendar to schedule your worry for another day?

Ultimately, the work is about presence

One of Nicole's challenges is sleep. She may go for weeks sleeping through the night, and then some small thing will set her off. She will wake up screaming approximately every hour. All through those nights, I hear the voices from other parents saying to let her cry herself to sleep. Having tried that a number of times, I know that her needs give her the capacity to scream for several hours, as some hidden anxiety turns off the inner need for rest. Even co-sleeping creates too much stimulation for her.

One night, after being woken up the third time in the night, I decided to try something different. I did not let her sleep in our bed, nor did I try to soothe her in bed. I gently spoke to her and assured her she was safe and loved. Something shifted in my heart and my perspective. Suddenly, my chaplaincy training kicked in.

One of the key teachings in my training as a resident chaplain was how to be at peace and present with someone or a family in utter turmoil. This is a lot harder than it may sound. It can be as challenging as shooting a free throw on the deck of a ship in a sea storm. While keeping our empathy turned on, we need to be moved emotionally and yet hold an inner stillness that gives the pain in the room permission to be. This is because when one person holds the calm in the room, the others can feel free to work through their own emotions. Eventually, the chaplain's own calm and self-control bring a sense of peace to the whole room. Calm is a contagious state of being.

So, I became my daughter's chaplain and heard her pain without thinking about how tired I was going to be the next day or how hard this was. Instead, I focused on being a peaceful presence for my child. I grabbed her bean bag and a few random blankets, and wrapped myself in pink on the floor. I told her that she needed to stay in bed but that I knew she was struggling. I would be present on the floor to remind her she was safe. She rested through the night, and I felt peace the next morning, even as my middle-aged body protested sleeping on the floor. After a week, her anxiety settled, and we were back in our own rooms, but the learning about presence helps whenever her anxiety comes back.

• • • • • • • • •

What are ways that you can practice being calm and present in the midst of your child's storm? How might this reassurance change your relationship?

Be the patience you want to see

I hate transitions. I hate that I cannot just beam my children from activity to activity like in Star Trek, or get them from the minivan into the house by wiggling my nose like Samantha in those old *Bewitched* episodes. No, we have to physically get from point A to point B, which means that someone is likely to throw a tantrum.

The other day my daughter fell asleep in the car. When we got home, she woke up and refused to leave the car. I was tired and tight for time, so I felt the inner need to fix the situation. I began to fantasize dragging her out and making her comply. But then I remembered that I was her example of patience. I stepped out of the van and breathed.

I told her that I was going to be nearby, but she needed to get out of the van herself. As I went around the corner of the house, I heard banging and loud crashes. I peeked around the car and saw the shrapnel of her attack on my sanity: a new book, a dog bowl, broken toys, and cashew nuts strewn all over the ground. My blood boiled. Now not only was I late, but I also had a mess to clean up. Have you ever been so angry that you could feel the veins on your neck throbbing? So angry that your teeth grind and your jaw locks like Rocky Balboa before a prize fight?

In the moment, I had to do two things to bring myself back.

First, I had to let go of my expectations of being on time. As a parent of two kids with special needs, I could no longer have perfect timeliness. It is simply not possible all of the time. Being early is too hard on the kids' patience, and being on time happens only when no one has a major tantrum.

The second thing I had to do was take care of myself physically. My heart was racing and my breath was short. My teeth were clenched. To reverse this, I needed to breathe ten times, just like we might teach our kids. I had to imagine my throat and my tongue softening.

Only after this did I let my daughter see my reaction. I walked over and simply said that she had lost a privilege and I was disappointed. I then just walked away.

Patience in the real parenting world is not easy. Patience is a lot easier to preach about than actually do. The reality is, the more we demonstrate patience, the more our kids will learn it. It might even be helpful for them to hear out loud how we are talking ourselves down from frustration to calm: "I am going to breathe right now. I am angry, so

I am going to slow down before I talk with you. I need to put myself in time-out and find my calm."

Patience is hard, and yet it seems to be teachable only through demonstration and practice. I have learned that I am a walking lesson on how to deal with frustration. I started to verbalize my process with her. "I am frustrated because ..." or "I am going to time-out because ..." and slowly my process sinks in. When the kids are at their most insane-making modality, I must be the patience I want to see.

• • • • • • • •

Do you model patience? What do you need to do for yourself in order to be the patience you want to see? What would you like your inner monologue be when you are frustrated?

Where is the real you?

I went through this phase—OK, I am always going back and forth on this—where, in my head, I want to say to people, "I have kids with special needs, so this frazzled person you are meeting is not really me. Wait until they are not around, and then you will really enjoy my company." This is never more true than when I am in the grocery store check-out line with my children. My inner monologue goes like this:

This isn't me! I am normally great at waiting in lines, but my kids are here, so please hurry up before someone explodes or tears up your display! If you could just let us through fast, I promise when I come back alone I'd love to chat about the weather and act normal. We are just trying to survive right now! Wait. Is she grabbing candy? AAGGHH! You'll meet the real me when the kids are not around!

The problem with this inner monologue is that it is rooted in resentment for having a child with special needs. We are in denial that our life has changed and we are not the same person as before we had children. We need to evolve and find a way to be less frazzled while we are with our kids. First, we need to do this because, if we are out and about with our kids often, this is how people will see us, even if we come in occasionally without our child. Secondly, if we are less frazzled only when our child is not around, our child will never get to know the better version of ourselves.

What have you given up of yourself with the excuse that now you have a child with special needs? What are the pieces of your pre-kid life that you need to pick back up?

If we probe our souls, we recognize the truth that there is still no excuse not to be ourselves. If we cannot dig deep and find the strength to give up this inner excuse, our kiddos will not have the joy of getting to know us—the real us. They will only know this neurotic adult who resents them for being human, let alone children, let alone children with special needs. Giving up the excuses frees you to find a new path to being who you really are: a calm, balanced, and caring human being, even when your kid is around. Dig deep and find your fun, expressive, and less frazzled self, and let that person show up when your child is around.

If you are having a hard time with this, consider borrowing from an ancient exercise of St. Ignatius, the founder of the Jesuits, a sect of Christianity that focuses on service and simple living. In the evening, play back your day like a movie in your mind. Go from hour to hour and retrace what happened. As you are doing this, pay attention to the state of your heart at each moment. What was happening in your heart? Were you nurturing a sense of peace at that time? Meditate on those moments that you would like to change. Open yourself up to God or the Universe and invite peace into that moment.

If you do this exercise daily for two to ten minutes, you will find that you are more mindful the next day about the state of your heart. You will feel less frazzled and more hopeful. Moreover, you may not only find your old, pre-kid self, but also find you are someone new entirely. And you may like this new person better. You may find you are a stronger, more resilient parent, because of your child. That will thaw your resentment and fuel the love that was always there.

• • • • • • • •

What have you given up of yourself with the excuse that now you have a child with special needs? What are the pieces of your pre-kid life that you need to pick back up?

This was never meant to be easy

My friends had concerns about their 21-year-old son and some of the life choices he was making. They shared with us that worrying about your children never ends. Parenting doesn't get easier; rather, the issues change with every stage.

For a long time I told myself that though things were hard now, later they would get easier. It was going to be easier once they sat up, or when they were out of diapers, or when they turned four. With special needs kids, however, it seemed like I had been duped. Life was harder at every stage.

Then one day it hit me: this was not meant to be easy. When I wanted a family, it was partly for the idyllic idea of being a parent, but it was also for the challenge of stepping into a new role. I knew that parenting was not going to be easy. It was very, very hard, and that was why it was worth doing. Complaining about something being hard would be like the sculptors of Mt. Rushmore complaining that it was hard to sculpt outdoors. It was the challenge, the audacity of it, that was worth engaging.

So go sculpt yourself the childhood of a kid with special needs. Even if it never feels like a choice to you, recognize that you make the choice to parent at your best every day.

• • • • • • • • •

What would it mean to think of yourself as someone living an extraordinary life, rather than a burdened one? What would it mean to claim the challenges before you as worthy of your extraordinary skills?

Perfection used to make you look good. Now it just makes you look like scrambled eggs.

As a kid, my own struggle with ADD had made it hard to be on time. Chronic tardiness had eroded my self-esteem, and I was determined as an adult to move past those feelings.

Before kids, after years of effort, I reached a semblance of perfect punctuality. If there was a meeting, I was always the one who arrived ten minutes early, twiddling my thumbs and feeling the euphoria of being prepared and balanced at the start of discussions. Then I had kids, two of which have special needs. Now being on time is more of a rarity. This is partially because being early means struggling to help the kids wait for their therapies, gymnastics, or whatever. But I still have the feeling that I should be on time. I often kill myself on the altar of punctuality.

The other day, I realized that I could get my wife, Joy, to work on time, Michael to his class on time, but Nicole was always late. This is because my son and daughter have classes that start at the same time. So, I would run like a madman from one of the end of the school, dropping my son off, to the other with my daughter to get her to class. If anyone said hi, I would ignore them and keep running. I even noticed that the clocks on each side of the school were not the same. His side was four minutes slow, and hers was about three minutes fast. This meant that the best we could do was be seven minutes late! One day, a teacher mentioned that we were always late, lighting my insecurity like a Roman candle. Wanting to get the clocks synchronized, I looked like a crazy man as I tried to convince the staff of the school that this mattered. The reality was that I was the only parent with two kids with special needs on two ends of the school. No one cared that I was late except the insecure kid inside of me.

When we try to keep up our perfection while we have a child with special needs, we end up stressed, and instead of looking competent, we just look like crazy. Poach your perfection and learn to wear a humble face, even if it gets egg on it.

· · · · · · · ·

What is one area of your day that is impossible to perfect? What would it mean to your sanity to relax your expectations in this area?

Try to be prepared, but don't stress when you are not

The other day, I found myself at home with Nicole and Michael when I realized that I had failed to plan for their special diets. They were hungry and getting antsy. I did not have any food in the house they could eat, not even my backup gluten-free/dairy-free muffins. I decided to make some fun out of it. "Let's go get a hot dog!"

Yay! I made a big deal out of the fact that hot dogs were on the horizon, if we could only get in the car, preferably with clothing and shoes.

At the hot dog stand, we find out that all the dogs have gluten in them, which won't work for my kids. I think, no big deal. We'll just walk across the way and get hot dogs from the Whole Foods grocery. I know they have the dogs that we need, and I can get a few things. The kids are helping me at Whole Foods, where I get additional items, when my daughter screams because some pears have fallen out of her junior-sized shopping cart.

I finally get to the hot dog section, only to find that they have discontinued the one brand of hot dogs that meet my kids' dietary restrictions. I now have to attempt to convince my children that the buns would be enough, simply an impossible sell at this point. I curse under my breath and ask myself in an internal scream, *Why didn't I have a muffin?*

But here is the thing. My kids rallied. I gave them the buns with some of our special cheese, and they were OK. I just assumed they would not be flexible. Against all odds, here they were, twice-rejected, and still content.

I have started to understand that I cannot predict how my children will react. I can live in the moment and deal with things as they come. I can also be less hard on myself when I don't have a gluten-free muffin when I need one. Just breathe and get through it.

• • • • • • • •

What are the voices in your head that assume the worst of your exceptional child? How many times is the actual stress less than you would have predicted?

The perfect storm

Joy said she missed the old me. She asked, "What happened to that person who was so optimistic and always looked for the good?"

I couldn't find that person for a while. I have since come to believe that there is a perfect storm of stressors that can weaken my optimism. The first wind in my perfect storm is insufficient rest. When my kids get up in the middle of the night for several nights running, I just can't function with my own special needs, and my life runs like an advertisement for ADHD medication. I get floaty in my head, and my thoughts are like sticky notes with no glue.

The second wind in my perfect storm is isolation. There is something about having kids with special needs that makes friends run for the hills. That isolation is a wind that can knock you down.

The last wind is the hitting and yelling that often comes from kids who are developmentally delayed. This negative energy would be almost laughable if it weren't so painful.

When this triad converges, I get negative and passive-aggressive. My own personal, perfect storm. I have found that when I feel overwhelmed, it is when all three are blowing at the same time. My way out is to block out one of these winds. When I can get enough rest, or find community, I can handle the other stressors.

The good news is we don't have to fix everything, just one of the stressors that creates the perfect storm. Before we know it, the real us is back in the game, and we can once again be labeled as the eternal optimist. Or at least people can stand to be around us again.

• • • • • • • •

What winds create your perfect storm? What is one wind that you can calm right now?

Don't care as much about making friends

When my family first moved into our new neighborhood in Portland, I felt a lot of pressure to establish a community for my family and especially for my kids. I invited some of the neighbors with kids the same age to our house and scanned the playground for any potential friends for our kiddos. Each effort, it seemed, ended either with people never inviting us back or with my kids ending the playdate with a tantrum. To be honest, a lot of the time, it felt like people stepped back and did not engage with us at all. I am Indian-American, my spouse is blind and uses a guide dog, and my kids are African-American. Plus, my kids tended to scream on the way out of the house every morning. These things together made it a little scary to connect with us for the average Joe or Joanne.

Then it turned out that we needed to move, to another house, in another neighborhood.

In our new place I was less engaged in trying to connect with the neighbors. I did not really care if they liked us or not. I had no investment in connecting, because my efforts hadn't worked before. Then, out of the blue, people started talking to us. They seemed interested. It seemed that when I stopped caring, my spirit began to loosen and let go. The freedom I felt, even in my disconnect, created a kind of magnet. The truth is that most people care what others think of them. But when we let go of our expectation, it leaves room for new possibilities. And that reality creates an environment of freedom around us.

People are always attracted to freedom. When we feel internal freedom, it spreads out its own field of magnetism, and suddenly people enter into our lives. The disconnect also allows us to open ourselves to unlikely friendships. That is the real surprise, and no matter how different you feel with your special needs kids, there are always people out there who are excited to befriend your family. Just let go and give them time.

• • • • • • • • •

Imagine that you are going to move from your current community in a month, freeing you from trying to fit in. How would that freedom change your level of anxiety?

Enjoy your kid

There are times when my son and daughter drive me nuts. The back talk, the behavior issues, and their unique needs are enough to give me fantasies of packing a U-Haul and taking off. When I get in this mindset, it is easy to see my kids as problems that need to be fixed so I can survive, maybe even enjoy family life someday. But the shift came for me when I realized that it was my role to genuinely enjoy my kids for who they were. I know. I know. Enjoying a kiddo who is screaming and acting in perpetual unrest is a bit of a contradiction in terms. Even so, stay with me for a moment.

When I made the shift to appreciate their strengths, I began to see the sacred in who they were, even with their back talk and yelling. They were a gift. When I began to look for the good in them, my fatigue was cut in half. My son has low energy and is hard to motivate at the park, but he is the perfect companion at a coffee shop. My daughter is so busy and tactile that you can't go anyplace where there are breakables, but take her to an amusement park and there is never a better companion.

When I could appreciate their strengths and find ways for those to shine, I genuinely enjoyed my children. When I enjoyed them, they started to add to my energy and optimism, rather than deplete them. It was a new day.

• • • • • • • • •

What are your child's strengths? When do they shine? How can you pick and choose your actitivites to emphasize these strengths?

A really bad morning does not always mean a really bad day

In the unpredictable world of special needs, it can be tempting to gain a sense of control by trying to forecast what kind of behavior to expect based on what happens in the morning. It is like looking at the sky in the morning, sticking up your wet finger, and forecasting the weather for the day.

I live in the Pacific Northwest, and I have learned you cannot judge the day's weather by what you see in the morning. It could be a downpour at dawn, but literally out of the blue (or even a little blue), sunshine is always possible.

The same is true when we have kids with special needs. When we start off the day badly, it is easy to assume that the day is shot. We already are spent, and it is 9 a.m. How are we going to make it through the day? When we have one of those mornings when the transitions just won't work, it is easy to spiral into the negative and lose a sense of possibility. It is easy to shrug our shoulders and give up on the myriad of tasks that are before us.

If, when you are reading this, you are having one of those mornings, don't go there. Instead of calling the entire day a loss, consider breaking up your day into three-hour mental chunks.

The reality and beauty of kids is that every few hours is like a new day for them. They could have a tantrum for the record books and then pull out behavior that makes us smile. I have finally learned that what starts out as their worst day may actually be their best day in disguise. I have to let go of my internal forecasting to let that possibility occur. When I allow them to have a really good day, even with the mother of all tantrums earlier, it frees us all to celebrate. And isn't celebration what feeds your soul?

● ● ● ● ● ● ● ●

What can you do to set off your morning from your afternoon? Can you have a cup of tea or listen to the radio for two minutes to reboot and reclaim hope for the next few hours? Do you need to write out your resentment and rip it up? What works best for you to turn off your internal forecaster?

When other people comment on how good your kids are, let yourself believe it

My kids do this annoying thing that is common with kids with their issues: they can be perfect angels for short bursts of time.

A woman down the street offers drop-in day care. Michael has almost never been in trouble there. He is able to hold his explosions in and save them for Daddy and Momma later in the day. The caregiver always tells me that he was a perfect angel for her. Of course, I think. He is allowed to watch TV, eat cookies, and play with toys he does not have. And, his issues make it possible to fake it for a little while. I am happy that he is able to stay with a caregiver; that is not always the case, as I shared earlier.

However, I always sneered internally whenever she said this at pickup. I think a part of my insecurity as a parent made me wish I had her skills. She has been caring for kids this age for a lot of years. Moreover, a lot of the other kids she watches respond well to rules. The good behavior of peers often helps kids with verbal processing issues, like

Michael. Michael cannot always process verbal commands, but he *can* copy other kids.

On the other hand, I do not give my son the credit he deserves. He has accomplished something special, every time he makes good choices. He reminds me of an angry John McEnroe, the tennis legend notorious for his court-side tantrums. Yet, every once in a while, like McEnroe, my son deserves applause for hitting an ace, even when it was not with me. When I was able to let go of some of my insecurity and just enjoy that he could be an angel, I was free to see him in all his potential.

He needed to see me proud, and, more than that, I needed to practice that for my own soul.

Whenever we imagine ourselves in the presence of angels, our energy shifts, and we again rest into possibility and hope. That hope is better than any trophy for the parent who wants to see their child hit a winner ever once in a while.

• • • • • • • •

Who are the people with whom your child can fake it for a while? What can you do to celebrate that success rather than resent it?

Don't whine ... in front of just anyone

Part of the challenge of having kids with special needs is that it is easy to get snide around people who have typically-developing kiddos. I remember seeing two parents at a baby store, overwhelmed by their two-year-old, who was barely acting up at all. I wondered why they were stressed in such a low-key situation. It's hard to sympathize with parents who are beleaguered by what we might define as benign challenges.

My daughter Nicole and I used to belong to a play group. I loved the parents and thought highly of them. But as my daughter's special needs intensified, I found that when they would whine together about how hard life was, I felt kind of angry inside. What did they have to complain about? Up once in the night? Try four times a night! Can't go to a restaurant? What about trying to brush your teeth or take a shower?

When I complained, my stories were so over-the-top that they shut down the conversation. Of course, though I was trying to gripe and grumble along with the other parents, it sounded like I was one-upping everything they said. Instead of bonding, it caused a dissonance in our relationship, and they stopped sharing with me.

Finally, I learned not to whine—at least, not with just anyone. I began to realize that my life experience pulled me away from the center of society and isolated me. I discovered I needed to be silent when typical families complained. I needed to acknowledge that the issues overwhelming them were legitimate parenting experiences. I had to pretend that their issues were paralleling my own. But I also needed to find community with whom it was OK to whine a little bit.

Finding the right community to whine with does two magical things. First, it lets us fake it with people with typical families, and, second, it keeps our whining to a minimum, because it is restricted to those times that people are really ready to listen. We feel support, and our subconscious is told that it will get time to complain, but not all the time and not with just anyone.

• • • • • • • •

Do you have any support groups in your community? Have you found Facebook groups or other online forums where you can feel free to whine productively? Do you have a friend with a child with special needs to talk with once a month?

Be happy now

What a difference these changes in attitude and perspective have made in my life and my spirit. I am no Jesus or Dali Lama, but in contrast with where I was, there has been significant progress. I was hurting and sinking before I realized the simple truth: my happiness could not depend on my children getting better. In fact, even if they got worse, I needed a new capacity to be happy.

It did not mean that every new therapy did not give me hope, or that every good day did not make me think maybe we had weathered another developmental milestone. What it meant was that I had a new spiritual assumption. Being happy has nothing to do with comfort or progress. It has everything to do with acceptance and peaceful living.

When we operate with these assumptions, we can accept ourselves and our children as they are. Acceptance takes off the pressure. At the same time, it gives us back the responsibility for our own spiritual care.

Before kids, I knew that spiritual self-care was important to the quality of my life. I prayed daily, belonged to a prayer group and a weekly collegial care group, and worked in a homeless shelter. I guess I looked quite holy for a while. Yet once I had kids, I lacked the energy even to read anything remotely spiritual. The kids sapped my energy and time, and I was losing my connection to my beliefs. If only the kids were in a better place and more manageable, I thought, then I could feel spiritually grounded again. Then maybe, in turn, I would be centered and whole again.

I finally realized that when you have kids with special needs, you have to *act as if* you are grounded and spiritually whole.

Then, in a kind of crazy trick of the soul, the universe says, "Because you are grounded, I'm going to start to let this work feed your soul." And the work of raising kids becomes itself a spiritual grounding.

There is a reason that great spiritual thinkers like Henri Nouwen gained spiritual depth by working with people with special needs. People with special needs expand our soul, because those needs force us into humbler places with ourselves. But here is the trick: until we operate from a grounded place, we cannot see this truth or accept it. We continue to be buried in resentment.

My trick? Fake it until I make it. In time, other spiritual practices, like holy reading or community, will find their places in the patchwork of life. Behave as if you were grounded already and soon your spirit will catch up, and parenting might begin to feed your soul.

• • • • • • • •

What would being grounded look like for you? What are the kinds of things you would say? How would you be with your family? What is one thing that you could change in your manner right now?

Live life like you are blind at a busy intersection

My wife, Joy, has been blind from birth. Like most blind folks, she has taken many mobility lessons. An instructor from the State Commission for the Blind worked with her on using her cane and her hearing to cross an intersection safely. Many people wonder how a blind person knows when to cross the street. The answer is that they listen for the cars next to them to surge forward. It is called listening for parallel traffic. When there is enough traffic to hear a surge, the traffic forms a kind of automobile wall so that left-turners are not going to hit you when you cross through the intersection.

Parenting kids with special needs is a lot like crossing an intersection blind. You cannot see what is next because you can't rely on typical markers or age categories. We don't know when we should attempt the crossing.

But if we wait for some semblance of initiation from our children, we cross with that momentum. It is like hearing a parallel traffic surge and knowing it is time to cross. That momentum protects us from the expectations of the rest of society. We don't need to be able to see what is next. We just need to listen and wait. And if we just aren't sure, there is always another signal cycle coming.

Having the trained patience and listening abilities of a blind person with good mobility skills would do all parents some good.

• • • • • • • •

What can you do to let go of your expectations of the timing of your child's developmental milestones? What is one thing you are pressing too hard to accomplish too soon? What strengths have you failed to notice?

Your family is weird, so get over it

I often see bumper stickers and signs saying "Keep Portland Weird." Come to think of it, I have seen that same logo in Houston and Berkeley, so I am pretty sure the weird motto is copied from city to city. My guess is that every city has idiosyncrasies, an identity that residents take pride in. The weird motto defends what is precious and delightful about that city. If that is true for cities, the same could be true for families as well.

I used to be self-conscious about my family, the way we looked so out-of-the-box. At some point I turned around and declared to myself that we were weird, and I was OK with that. Moreover, I realized that if I tried to pretend we weren't, I would be rejecting something that made us unique. Even more than that, our weirdness was a gift to every street we lived on and to each store we attempted to visit as a family. We were the unique family that made living near us unlike any other place. Keep this family weird!

The tough part, of course, is the gossip and the whispers we hear around us, the people who slowly move us out of their playgroups, or the ones who are annoyed with our difference. Even more troublesome is the discomfort of people, often our own friends and relatives, who struggle with the weirdness as affecting their self-image. It's their uneasiness that can be damaging to our family's spirit.

There is no secret way to make this less painful or awkward. What has helped me is to embrace weird in general, to think of us as whimsical works of art, unique and beautiful. Precious. Valuable. And though the critical voices remain, they don't get to be the predominant internal voice. Just like any work of art, let people have their opinions, but make sure you get to apply the right frame.

● ● ● ● ● ● ● ●

What makes your family weird? Is there a playful way that you can name it and celebrate it as a family?

Be patient with friendships

Our next-door neighbors seemed snobby. It seemed that as soon as they saw we had kids with special needs, they backed off and did not want to connect. The sad part was that our kids were so social. They kept saying hello, inviting their children to come over to play. But they did not get invited back over. No surprise. Our kids were pretty loud, even intimidating.

Later we found out that our neighbors were going through a separation and possibly divorce. They were hurting and did not want other people to see it. For nearly a year, I just assumed it was our difference that was keeping the kids from being invited over. Now I understand—I do not know what is going through people's heads when they keep their distance.

For parents of kids with special needs, it is hard to remember that people with "normal" families struggle to keep marriages together, to raise responsible kids, to make it through each day.

Now, for the sake of my own soul, I start with a new assumption. Other people can be snobby, but we can choose not to be. Living with that openness and grace can change everything. When our neighbors' separation became public, they started to invite our kiddos over. We are not sure if playdates will ever turn into a family friendship, but they are a start.

• • • • • • • • •

What are the assumptions you make about how other people see you? Can you give a relationship with another family a little more time to develop?

Give grace to your partner first

Adding children to any relationship means added strain and tension. Having kids with special needs has to be one of the greatest stressors on a relationship. When the screaming, hitting, physical caregiving isn't getting to you, the lack of restful sleep will do you in. You feel like you can literally kiss that sex life goodbye. Neither is getting what they need in the relationship.

Often in these situations, people drift apart, and no one else hears of it until it is too late and the relationship is beyond repair. Sometimes being in community with people when the marriage/partnership is approaching the rocks helps a couple stay together. But the isolation of having kids with special needs also means you aren't connected anymore. Special needs are like a tourniquet that cuts off your contact with outside support. Slowly, without a community to keep you in check, your primary relationship starts to die.

My relationship with my spouse started to suffer when date night was compromised every time the sitter got sick or was out of town. When we did have a date, we would use the time to problem-solve and figure out how to help our kids. While important work, talking about the kids for hours on end is neither romantic nor truly bonding.

The turnaround in me happened when I realized that date night was not enough. I needed to find a way to connect with my spouse every day. We found that connection in taking hot baths together. We did that every day and, despite a hefty water bill, we have done some remarkable repair. The baths were only possible when I gave up my routine of plopping down in front of the TV and blocking out the world at the end of my crazy day as a stay-at-home dad. I had nothing more to give, but zoning out with my spouse and even talking, rubbing her shoulders, making things good again between us was like an awakening. It was like my soul was being baptized into new life, and I was sharing it with my spouse.

It may be that baths are not your thing. You might prefer bike rides, looking at a book together, or sitting with a glass of wine while listening to soft music. It does not have to be much. There is power that comes with an almost daily attempt to connect a little. In fact, small daily efforts may do a lot more in the long run than a big, flashy effort later on.

Save your marriage or relationship by taking time each day to connect. Of course, a weekly date night on top of that is a great romantic connection as well. Certainly it is cheaper than couple's therapy later on, if you feel you need to justify the expense.

If you have a relationship, tend it a little every day. Just like a garden.

• • • • • • • •

What is something you could do with your partner that would take ten minutes or less to enjoy with each other? How can you begin to add those moments into your daily lives? What would need to fall away to make that time possible?

Be ready to say hello spiritually

Part of supporting my spouse of late is to take her to her Dragon Boating practices by the Willamette River in Portland, Oregon. In Dragon Boating, people paddle in crews and race down the river.

We pack up the kids and guide dog, and go to the river every Saturday. For two hours, I must occupy the kids by the river and hope I can keep them from jumping in! This means navigating crazy impulses, fits of rage, and strange sensory needs, all in the name of family fun.

One Saturday, I was particularly annoyed that the kids had decided to say hello to a woman who was peacefully meditating by the river. I decided to simply ask the woman if it was OK if they said hello.

"Yes," she said. Big mistake on her part.

The kids asked their never-ending follow-up questions. "What is your name? What are you doing? Are you praying?"

She said, "I am meditating."

"What is medi-a-ing?"

"It is trying to be present."

At this point, I interjected, "She is trying to be ready to say hello to whatever comes."

This was my way of trying to explain how she was concentrating but not lingering intentionally on any thought. Her attention was always expansive and versatile with what was before her. She was ready for an aha moment to come any time, from anywhere.

She smiled at my layperson's interpretation. She said she was looking at the grass, and now she was enjoying my kids. Enjoying them! Wow!

She invited them to ring her Buddhist bell. It was a truly memorable parenting moment.

I think it is hard to be ready to say hello to such interactions with the public. It can be easy to stay back, trying to stop the kids from interacting too much with society, especially if they have behavioral issues.

Yet if we can get over our fear of interaction, we may be ready to say our own hellos to the world. Sometimes this will backfire, but when we run into someone else who is also ready to say hello to whatever comes, the moments can be profound for everyone.

• • • • • • • •

What are ways that you intentionally shut out the outside world from your family? What would happen if you decided to risk openness more frequently instead? What are the spiritual experiences you would love to invite into your lives?

Keep a list of great experiences or sayings

I asked my daughter to bring her brother a peach. It took her a few minutes, but she delivered the peach to her brother. The only problem was the peach had little holes all over it. I asked my daughter why there were holes.

"I took all the bad parts off."

I asked what she did with all the bad parts. She took a moment before her reply. "I ate them."

This was one of those moments that made me smile, one that I treasured. I typed the conversation into my phone and later copied it to a file I keep on my computer. The file is like my own Twitter page, where I write one-liners from my kids.

I have also started to video my kids when they are having fun and play the films back at the end of the day. Capturing these moments on paper or video puts them on the front burner. There is something spiritually healing and satisfying in remembering good things about someone.

We all know this to be true at funerals. As a minister, I have been to a multitude of funeral and memorials and am constantly surprised at the variety of stories and communities involved. With all that variety, what does not change is the need for loved ones to speak about something positive. The people being honored all sound like saints, which of course is not likely. Yet, there is something healing in enjoying the good memories out of all the messy events that make up a lifetime.

Just like people at funerals, parents of kids with special needs are living with a kind of grief all the time. I remember trying to take Michael to gymnastics. While he screamed and threatened the other Lycra-laden tykes, I grieved that I did not get to sit on the viewing couch and read the paper like the other parents. Instead, I had to take my screaming child to the restroom to calm him.

When this kind of thing happens again and again, the combined grief can skew my relationship with my son. Yet when I capture the good moments and keep them in front of me on the hard days, the grief is easier to bear. It goes to the back of my mind, and I can enjoy the good memories being made in the present.

• • • • • • • •

How can you to record the good memories happening in your family life? A small notebook in the car, a portable recorder, your smart phone? Let go of perfection and do whatever works for you.

Your kids are not your self-portrait

When people see a child doing poorly in public, they look at the parent for an indication as to why that kid is struggling. Sayings like, "The apple does not fall far from the tree," reflect this common assumption.

I remember an incident at a restaurant. Our daughter was having a bad sensory day. She was under the table, then laying half her body on top of it within a few seconds. We quickly employed our techniques to help bring her back from the brink. Finally, I took her to the car so that she could cool off a bit. While Joy paid the bill, she overheard a conversation at the table next to ours, two women gossiping loudly about us, how our child was so poorly behaved, and what terrible parents we were.

The reality is that we were at our parenting best in this situation. We kept our cool, employed our plan together, and stuck to our guns with limits. Still, we were judged as if our child had no special needs and we had no parenting sense whatsoever.

Some of us can turn off other people's opinions. I know that my spouse has an easier time of this than I do. For me, it took more internal work to get to that state of mind.

For those wired to be self-conscious, some degree of separation from their children is necessary. I don't mean that we spend less quality time or are less involved emotionally. I mean that we need to separate our self-image from that of our special-needs child. We need to define a self-portrait that does not include a squirmy child in hand, a crying baby strapped on, or an angry teen texting in the background.

So how do we begin to break out of these negative spirals and move forward? I refused to let my children define who I was, positively or negatively. I could not judge myself, even my parenting, on whether my child was able to fit into others' expectations on a given day. That roller coaster was killing me.

I started my new self-portrait by taking a little time for grooming. I started the day fifteen minutes earlier, had a shower, and got dressed before anyone else. I combed my hair, shaved, and brushed my teeth. I even hired someone to help me update my clothes. While my kid would wear his pants backward and and his shirt inside out, I was not going to wear sweats with bed head. I looked great; I was a separate person from my kids.

I also started to keep my car cleaner when possible. My diaper bag was emptied more often. In short, when my kids were out of control, I could look at myself in the mirror and literally see that I was not falling apart. I could be proud of myself and teach that pride to my kids.

Moreover, internally, I began to feel that their ups and downs were not my own. I projected an image of self-control, and slowly I began to believe it.

That boost of self-esteem can shift the spiritual center of an entire family unit. When we look our best, it radiates that we are approachable and trustworthy, and that leads to unforeseen social possibilities. Do not underestimate the power of looking your best and being your own self-portrait.

● ● ● ● ● ● ● ●

What is one thing you could do to improve your appearance? What would a bit of professional grooming do for your confidence? Try to put yourself together before your first morning drop-off and see how it changes your self-image.

Religious beliefs should support your struggle, not undermine your self-worth

As a spiritual leader, I often hear the deep struggles of families. It troubles me when parents with an exceptional child say to me, "I must have done something wrong to have a child like this. God is punishing me."

The implication of such messages is that we are to blame for our less-than-perfect families. We can feel a sense of shame and wonder what we are doing wrong in our parenting.

The reality is that when it comes to special needs, such self-blaming talk is mistaken. There is no God or higher power who punishes people by giving them kids with special needs. God is there for strength and redemption, for healing and new purpose. God is never about tit for tat or evening the scales of justice through pain. We did not do anything wrong. Furthermore, our kids are beautiful and unique creations; they are not mistakes.

If you are part of a religious organization that teaches that your child is a result of anything but a positive miracle, then consider looking elsewhere for community. Religious beliefs should be a constant source of strength for you, not undermine your self-worth or that of your family.

• • • • • • • • •

What are the harmful beliefs that you have been holding on to? What are the communities that affirm your family? How can you spend more time closer to those people?

Smile and dismiss platitudes that don't affirm you or your child

When confronted with a painful situation, it is easy for all of us to rely on platitudes in order to have something safe to say. One platitude that I often hear when people learn we have two kiddos with special needs is, "God only gives you what you can handle." It is meant with deep kindness, but what does it really mean? That we should be able to handle whatever comes in life?

What if we cannot handle it? There have been times when my spouse and I gave up and threw our hands up in the air. Just this past week, when my son hit his school teacher, we felt we had totally failed our child. We had tried everything to help him find his calm, and he kept crossing that line. Sometimes it is really clear that our frustration is too great to handle.

When people run into something that they cannot handle, yet they try and try until they admit defeat, despair is the result. It is only when they admit they cannot manage, at least, not perfectly, that an opening allows other people to stand with you. I wish the platitude was this: "God only gives you burdens with multiple handles so others can grab one and share your load. You are not alone."

In fact, it may be good to have a platitude fixer going on silently in your mind. You can change the platitude to one that works better for you.

For example, if someone says, "Your child's special needs are a gift from God," you can change it in your mind to "Your needs are also important to God. God will put gifted people in your life to help. You will not need to be alone in this."

Or, "Let go and let God" can be changed in your head to "God will not let go of you!"

Whatever your beliefs and whatever the platitudes that drive you batty, just smile and change the phrase to one that gives you the strength you need. People mean well, but they don't always think about what is meaningful to you.

By the way, if any of these sayings give you strength as they are, that's fine, too. You know best what gives you the support you need for the days ahead.

· · · · · · · ·

Consider writing down a list of platitudes that drive you crazy. How would you rewrite them so they could affirm your family?

Live in grace

My three-year-old son said, "Mom, you are the best parent in the whole world!"

Smiling, I asked, "What am I, chopped liver?"

He said, "Dad, you are the best chopped liver in the whole world!"

Yes, at times, we are all chopped liver as parents. Some days, despite our best intentions, we are going to fail hard at raising our kids. Not too long ago, my daughter refused to have her hair done for the second morning in a row. Her beautiful African American hair was tangled and matted. I was embarrassed for her, and, to be honest, for all of us. I finally picked her up and started combing and braiding her hair.

She screamed, "Please don't do my hair!"

"Why not?" I asked.

"Because I don't want you to do it." Perfect four-year-old logic.

My blood boiled, and I put her onto the floor, raising my voice and becoming a two-year-old before her very eyes. After a word from my spouse, I put both of us in time-out.

On days like these, I wonder, who am I to write about parenting? I am no better a parent than anyone else! But then, I think, this is why I write. I write because I am not the parent I should be, and that is OK.

I am starting to believe that parenting is not about doing everything correctly, or even loving children perfectly. Parenting is a divine practice of grace, a constant reminder that we all fall short.

The Laurie Berkner Band is a children's music group that my son loves. One of their songs, "I'm not perfect," goes:

I'm not perfect, no I'm not
I'm not perfect, but I've got what I've got
I do my very best, I do my very best
I do my very best each day
But I'm not perfect
And I hope you like me that way

Whenever my kids request this song, I am reminded of grace. Living in grace is a practice that gives other people permission to do the same. Forgiving ourselves daily is perhaps the best internal prayer we could offer. It is saying, I am not meant to be perfect. Being raised by someone perfect would be hell.

We are supposed to bring our best each day, but that is always changing, and that is OK. Being raised by people who have flaws is OK. Sometime the parent is in time-out, and that is important for kids to see, too.

What are ways that you can live in grace? How can you use your flaws as teaching moments for your child?

Forgive your friends and family for not always fathoming your life

I have some friends who are naturally kind-hearted, and I love them deeply, but it is hard for them to comprehend my family's day-to-day life.

They wanted to go on a children's cruise and asked if we wanted to go with them. Having two preschool children with sensory needs, I could not envisage going on a cruise with its lights, noise, people, and stimulation. I imagined my daughter jumping off the boat just to act out her defiance. Restaurant dining at every meal would be the unhappiest place on earth. Also, we were financially broke from all the therapies and interventions for the kiddos. I appreciated the invitation, but at the same time felt frustration that once again our special needs would probably exclude us, at least until the children were ready.

Beyond missing out on some special occasions, one of the deepest sources of pain I have heard from parents of kids with special needs is that almost all the people they dreamed would be around are not. Many people take a step back from situations that are hard or unpredictable. When we most need help from family and friends, they are often not there. We feel alone and abandoned.

If it takes a village to raise to raise a child, it feels like kids with special needs require a metropolis. And yet, here we are, feeling more alone than ever. What can we do with these feelings spiritually? I think we must start with an internal stance of forgiveness. Especially if we have abandonment issues, we cannot allow resentment to take over. Once we have forgiven our parents, our siblings, our friends, we do best to let go of expectations.

Often they do not know they have stepped back. Having special-needs kids is such a paradigm-shifting, mind-bending experience that we forget how much we have changed. We have also left them, our support, behind. We are not the same people we once were, and since this happens in almost all families, this is not personal.

We also need to forgive ourselves for changing and distancing other people. If you feel like your friends and family don't empathize, and you can't push them to change, give yourself permission to give up for a while. You may be surprised how taking the pressure off gives them the time to catch up and become an advocate. People change and learn on their own, and sometimes we are astonished at the sudden transformation.

• • • • • • • •

How can you let go of your expectations? Who needs your forgiveness?

It takes a village to raise a child, but it might *not be* your *village*

It does take a village to raise a special-needs child, but it may not be our village. What I mean is, that we will slowly find people who are comfortable with the craziness of our families. If we believe our children are created and are whole just as they are, that, indeed, we are thus whole as a family, then we must accept ourselves. Once we have accepted who we are as a family, another village will rise up around us. The right support and encouragement will fill in the gaps.

My spouse and I adopted our children, and, living into that role as an adoptive parent, I have learned that all relationships are in the end adoptive. People do not have to be related to be family. Friends do not have to be of the same age or background. Friends are everywhere to be found. Find support groups, get online, just be real with who you are, and you will not be alone. A new village will be there to fill in the gaps, and the old village may find its way back as you find your own grounding.

• • • • • • • •

What other villages are around you that you have not yet explored? What would it take to add new circles of community into your life? Is there a religious community or a support group you could join? Is there a family you could meet through a therapist or early intervention specialist?

Rituals matter

One of the things that I most enjoy about my Jewish friends is the degree to which they practice rituals. The Seder meal, for example, is a deepening of the remembrance of the Passover, a time that the ancient Hebrew people came together and escaped slavery. Furthermore, they truly became a people. Rituals such as the Seder meal have kept them vibrant as a people, even after diaspora.

One of the difficulties of parenting is that all the little rituals that made us feel sane are disrupted, at least for a while. My morning ritual of a cup of coffee, a nice walk, or a morning prayer are now pretty much obliterated. Even date night, a practice my spouse and I kept for over a decade, disappeared with the coming of a second child with special needs.

Rituals hold the possibility of spiritual wholeness. Without them, we can lose our grounding, our sense of who we are.

A ritual does not need to be religious to be spiritual. When we do something that holds meaning, it returns the meaning back to us just by our doing it. When we set the table for Thanksgiving, religious or not, it recalls all the other times we have done this. Even talking about setting the table for Thanksgiving may help us to recall people and places we haven't thought about for some time.

Sometimes our children identify their own rituals and ways of holding memory. My daughter found her stuffed baby otter. For me, it is just another stuffed animal among many, but the otter reminds her of visiting the aquarium when she was two years old. Children are masters of using props and rituals to remember what is important. They often remember what toys were given by grandparents or other loved ones.

One of the spiritual practices that has helped me is making rituals around the most basic things in life. We have celebrations around successes and transitions.

For instance, when I pick up the kids from preschool, I often have something waiting for them on their seats—a sticker, a healthy snack, or occasionally something particularly red-letter. It makes coming home momentous, and it makes it easier to get them into the car.

When they wake up in the morning, I insist they ask, "Good morning, how did you sleep?" even if they know that our sleep was horrible because of their rough night. We do a victory lap in the yard for a good day, or we keep mac and cheese a special treat for when the baby sitter comes.

I used to think of these things as bribes, but when I changed my perspective to more of a spiritual practice, I began to see these celebrations as rituals with real power to bring happiness into the household. Having some control over the rituals also gave me a creative outlet that did not depend on the behavior of the kiddos. It allowed me to get a snapshot of a moment of a regular family life, or at least what I imagine it to be.

Also, rituals can be just for you. For me, starting to write this book was a renewed ritual. Taking time to hunch over a computer and mull over my thoughts is an activity I used to do as a full-time minister. Sitting in a coffee shop and listening to someone else's music changes my perspective and sets the neurons buzzing, reminds me that I am still an adult with a brain. Somehow, when I put on the apron and start my stay-at-home parent routine, that's easy to forget. Rituals matter.

• • • • • • • • •

What was your favorite ritual B.C.—before children? What is one you can bring back today?

You are getting paid for this

Some of the greatest people I have met are the various speech therapists, occupational therapists, and you-name-it therapists that have worked with my kids. What I sometimes envy is their immense amount of energy and patience.

I often think that the kind of attention these experts give to my children is not sustainable for me. Even if I ordered take-out for every meal and hired someone to clean, I would still be left with shuttling the kids and doing laundry, etc. There is no way that I could be that engaged with them all the time. I just don't have the energy or emotional reserves.

It is sometimes helpful to imagine that I have just one hour with my kids. I pretend that I am the therapist and for the next hour, I will be paid for my work. I am a professional. So, when my kids struggle, I can say, "This is why I get paid the big bucks," and pretend I know exactly what to do, and that later I will get a chance to rest by the water cooler. Believe it or not, pretending I am a pro actually works. I am ready to get the job done, at least for an hour at a time.

● ● ● ● ● ● ● ●

Who are the professionals whose work you admire? What can you learn from their presence and energy?

Sabotage the negative slide

Some days are just harder than others. This past week my son came down all smiles in the morning and asked for a yogurt from the fridge. It was my sorry duty to inform him that we were out of yogurt. Would he like something else? He went berserk.

The next day, I had yogurt at the ready, and he asked for hot dogs. I wouldn't normally allow hot dogs for breakfast, so probably it was a good thing we were out of dogs, or I might have caved in. He let out a howl for the ages.

On these mornings it is easy to begin what I call my negative slide. The kids put me in a no-win situation, and I become like a child on a curvy slide at the park.

One disappointment in the morning, like the oatmeal being too hot for Michael, causes a cascade of events, leading to screaming in the car, multiple pee accidents, and projectiles in the minivan. Then I am discombobulated, and my negative mood adds to the feeling that everything is going downhill the entire day. I feel overwhelmed, and the tears and the stress take over.

What I am finally learning is that we can see the slide coming and simply say, No. I will not ride the slide today.

In the Bible, Jesus says, "Do not worry about tomorrow, tomorrow will worry about itself. Each day has enough trouble of its own" (Matthew 6:34). That verse used to mean to me, as a young single person, that my basic needs of living would be met each day. As a parent, I take it as a reminder to take each day one at a time, even break the day into several pieces, so one meltdown will not lead inevitably to another in my mind. If we do not mentally break apart our days and weeks, the negatives slide will begin. We need to focus on the moment at hand, and, as we engage with our child, let go of the past and the future emotionally.

The other day we went to the park, and there were chains blocking the curvy slide. The kids were surprised that a slide could be broken. It was cracked near the bottom. Anyone trying the slide would be harmed at the bottom.

So it is with our spirits. If we slide, we will get hurt and will not be as strong a parent as we could be. The resilient parent can recognize the slide early and put up mental chains in front of it. I will not slide today!

• • • • • • • • •

What are the things your child does that push your emotional buttons? What healthy food or positive readings could you keep on hand to sabotage your negative slide the moment it starts?

Focus less on the milestones and more on the stepping stones

Do you have an over-achieving personality? For over-achieving parents, it can be especially difficult to have a child with significant delays. Each missed milestone feels like we are failing as parents. But that negative spirit can only hurt ourselves and our children. What if we over-achieving types could focus on creating smaller success moments, rather than measuring overall output from our kids? Here is an example of a milestone that eluded my son for years.

I remember feeling I was the most horrible parent ever when I could not teach Michael to put on his shoes and socks. Fortunately, he had a very engaged early- intervention specialist, who explained to me that putting on his shoes and socks was too big a goal. I needed to let him do just a piece of the sequence, like holding open the sock or unfastening the shoe, and then burst into immediate, joyful applause if he did these small things. Over time, the other skills of sliding the sock on and closing up his shoe could be achieved. Letting him celebrate just a part of putting on his socks and shoes, such as just holding the shoe in the right way, helped him be less frustrated and more joyful about his progress.

By focusing less on milestones and more on stepping stones, the pressure to achieve was released, and Michael could be free to be a success at his own pace. Even more, though, as an over-achiever parent, I, too, was being retrained. In fact, one of the gifts of having children with special needs has been learning that success is more easily achieved by small steps coupled with mini-celebrations than by delaying all gratification until the ultimate goal is reached.

● ● ● ● ● ● ● ●

What are some milestones you've been dreaming about for your child? How could you help your child break down that goal? If you have a teen with ADHD, for example, instead of trying to get your child to be more organized and achieve a certain grade, could you celebrate the smaller stepping stone of using a calendar together and remembering all test dates for a semester? How would you both feel less stressed with a more acheivable goal?

Listen more when you are tired

It is so hard to listen to children for hours on end. The conversations are sometimes nonsensical to adults and more often just plain boring. With my own ADD, I find my attention drifting quickly. And yet there is nothing more precious to offer them than my attention.

The hardest scenario for me is when one of them has had a hard night and I am without rest. The fatigue turns me into a zombie struggling to put my own shoe on the right foot, let alone their shoes. I can hardly function, and my spirit gets depleted.

This is the time that I think just one thing: I need to listen. It will be harder to listen today, so I need to pay attention to that first. If the laundry is not done today, it will be OK, but if I fail to listen, I am failing to parent the way that I would like.

Of course, that does not mean that we need to be perfect with it, but focusing on listening, like a miracle, takes care of a lot of other concerns.

When listening, we give empathy when needed, and that creates a tone for the family. Listen first. Put a sign on the bathroom mirror that reads,

"Listening is your job." Do whatever gives you the drive to listen when you are tired.

Here is a story I like to share about the gifts of listening even when you are tired. One day I was especially tired and having a hard time listening to my daughter, who was constantly complaining. She came to me in distress, and all I could hear was something about sunglasses. I paused for a moment and made my best effort to listen. I asked her, "What is wrong with your sunglasses?"

She said, "I can't wear them. They are too wet."

"I don't understand. Wearing your sunglasses wet is perfectly fine."

She looked pained for a moment and replied, "But I dropped them in the toilet."

I was glad I had decided to listen with patience. If I hadn't, she would have probably flushed the toilet in retaliation, and I would have had to call an emergency plumber to fish out those sunglasses.

● ● ● ● ● ● ● ●

Who is the best listener you know? How does their listening positively impact your relationship? What would it mean to your child to have your full attention more often? What would it change in your family to never text or surf the internet while around your kids?

Go to a group six times
and don't miss one

Do you ever feel like a Halloween pumpkin left out on the porch a little too long? You look good on the outside, but inside you are empty, ready to collapse, and literally getting eaten up by something you can't even recognize? I have found myself especially like this when I set out to handle my kids on my own. Whenever I decide solo is better, I start out with a grin on my face but soon slide into a lopsided, unhealthy lifestyle—that is, if life doesn't kick me over first!

Having a child with special needs is much more like a pumpkin patch, where we are alive and connected to a community of care. Current psychological and sociological research says that the people who are most resilient have multiple circles of support, such as a support group or a spiritual community. Wouldn't you be better off connected to a patch that will give you life when the hard times come?

While connecting with people is, in theory, good for you, I'll admit it is hard to feel comfortable in a new religious community or a support group.

As good as any group of support is, the problem is that it is still a group, and groups seem to have a universal drawback. People tend to block out new members, often unintentionally, so you might go to a prayer group or a support group and simply give up after a time or two. You feel ignored or don't find the fellowship you need. There is nothing to hold you there. You leave and try to join another group.

You need to commit to a series of visits.

Having led multiple small groups, it has been my observation that the people who commit themselves to being present will get the most out of it. Often, group members are strangely cold the first few times a new person joins, but if the person attends regularly, the group warms to the new person. Unfortunately, most people do not stay in a group long enough to get to this sudden warmth. My advice is to find a circle of support in person, or even online, and commit to at least six sessions in a row before you decide if it is a fit.

I had this experience with a support group of other parents of children with special needs. I remember going the first time and realizing that almost no one would talk with me. I came a second time and again, no one spoke with me. The third time, it was a little better, but I was about ready to give up. I was a different gender from everyone else in the group and older than some. It was also clear that others continued to socialize outside of the group and I was not invited.

Normally, I would have looked for another group. However, remembering my own experience in leading many small groups, I realized that it might just take more time. I came the fourth time, and, all of a sudden, everyone in the group spoke with me as if I were a lifelong friend. This is often what happens in breaking into a new group. Nothing. Nothing. Then complete acceptance. I committed to not missing a session for nearly a year. Out of that group came inspiration for writing this book, deep, lasting friendships, and people whose children could be a new community for my children.

• • • • • • • • •

Are there any groups you have tried that might warrant some more visits? Is there a faith community that a friend attends that might work for you? Could you ask the friend to attend with you?

There is no quota for hard life stuff

My wife is blind, and we have known many blind friends. People often think that being blind is the worst that can happen to you. But the reality is that plenty of people live great, even extraordinary lives, while not being able to see a thing. The idea that blind people live lesser lives is utterly false.

I have also learned from my spouse of sixteen years that having a disability or dealing with something tough doesn't curtail the advent of new challenges. People with disabilities are not somehow immune to further disaster. This is like thinking that just because someone occupies a wheelchair, he might not have a heart attack, or that someone who is blind can't become HIV positive.

The same is true for families who have children with special needs. Just because things are hard does not mean that no further harm can come. There is no quota for how hard life can get or feel. This may sound like a real downer.

So, here is some vitamin D, a little sunshine on that cloudy thought. The realization that we are not immune from further harm can be helpful.

We realize that we are like everyone else. We have as many of the same struggles—aging parents, job loss, or a struggling marriage. We have a lot more in common with typical families than we might realize. We should never feel we have a monopoly on life's challenges; plenty of people have more going on than we can imagine.

When you know that the universe can hand you much worse, you can be grateful for only having to deal with your kids' special needs. You might not be thrown for a loop when bad things happen and you already feel spent.

As I write this, both my father and my mother-in-law have aggressive forms of cancer. I am worried a lot more about that cancer than I am about how hard my kid's special needs are. Only now do I realize how much I would give to worry only about my kids' special needs. The special needs stuff is hard, but it is not as scary as our parents' cancer. Isn't it funny how those special needs can feel so big until life slams into you like a Mack truck on black ice?

When we see those extra hard things as perspective changers, rather than as the things that break us emotionally, we can keep positive and not lose energy for the parenting challenges before us.

• • • • • • • •

Are there any hard things going on in your life that have nothing to do with your exceptional family? What would it mean to think of these things as perspective changers, not the things that will break you? If nothing else is stressing you right now, how can you have an attitude of gratitude that life is hard but it could be worse?

Screw your courage to the sticking place, and then play to their strengths

One day I found myself unexpectedly with an empty pantry and freezer. Out of extreme necessity, I decided to brave a grocery trip with all of my children.

Planning to keep my kids engaged, I chose a store with those little kid-sized grocery carts. Bad decision—Nicole and Michael thought it would be fun to bash those carts together. Eventually we made it to the check-out counter, and that's when true chaos ensued. All that tempting candy! Four little hands grabbed contraband faster than I could put it back. I had to walk out without my groceries with two screaming children. Humiliated, tired, and frustrated does not begin to describe my aggravated state. Plus, I had no supplies for the week.

I was never taking the children to the store again! Then, after my own mental time-out, I thought about what a trip to the grocery store could mean for the kids if we just handled it differently. They could learn about healthy food and have some ownership in the supplies I gathered. This errand was about learning, a purpose higher than getting things done.

Slowly, I psyched myself back up. How could their special needs be met? I decided that in order for the kids to be successful, I needed to keep the time in the store to no more than ten minutes. I could get only a few things at a time, and I needed to have a reward for the kids each time. They needed success. In order to get groceries, I was going to have to go two or three times a week for short bursts. I shuddered at the idea of going back with my children, but I screwed my courage to the sticking place, and, amazingly, when I played to their strengths, they succeeded, and we could buy groceries, a little at a time.

● ● ● ● ● ● ● ●

What is really important that your child experience? Why is it so important, and is there a way to break it down so that it is doable for your child? How can you play to your child's strengths?

An attitude of gratitude

OK, an attitude of gratitude is not an original idea. I have read many reminders that an attitude of gratitude is a way to spiritual fulfillment. A nice sentiment, but what if you're too exhausted to write a gratitude list at the end of the day? What happens when we are truly lost in "pity city" and want to stage our own occupy movement there?

The way out of "pity city" is to start with an attitude of gratitude for those who are supportive. For me, it starts with the amazing people who work with kids with special needs. The fact that my son's speech teacher takes his punches and still cares for him is a small miracle, and I have gratitude for the emotional maturity and effort that takes.

So how does one show gratitude to these people? First, and this may seem unspiritual, we need to make sure they are paid for their work. This means following up with insurance and paying ahead of time. It also means valuing their time in tangible ways. It may not always be possible to be punctual, but making the effort means a lot to them, because they understand what it takes for you to get anywhere on time.

I noticed flowers on the desk at Sensory Kids, a therapy center in Portland where I'd brought Michael. While waiting for our appointment, I asked the staff where the flowers came from. Someone had given the flowers as gratitude for intensive work done with their son. I remember thinking what a thoughtful and life-giving gift that was. I wondered how they managed to get on the phone, pick them up, and transport them without their child tearing them apart. Those flowers were grace for everyone who came in that day. Such an act of gratitude sets the tone for everyone.

One other thing: when we are busy being positive with an attitude of gratitude, we have less time to complain about the negative stuff. We give less attention to those who have harmed us and instead lean into the relationships that are currently healthy in our life. If you want to be resilient as a parent, spend more and more of your energy being thankful for the positive people around you.

• • • • • • • •

How might you start to show gratitude to the people who are supporting you right now? Who would be first on your list?

Compassion counts

There is an old story I once heard about a man who is approached by a king in a mythical kingdom. The king asks the poor man for some rice. The man is so angry that the king has asked him for something that he gives the king just five grains of rice. The king responds by giving him five grains of gold. The man, in despair, says, "If I had known what he would give me, I would have given him it all."

The story speaks to me, because as parents with exceptional kids, it can feel like we have nothing left to give. We can feel angry when people ask anything of us. We perceive we are being asked to give up our already negligible spare time.

Yet, for me, helping others has been a surprisingly positive experience. An adoption worker asked if I could support another family with a kiddo with special needs. Somehow, time opened up, and I found more energy to be present for them. The conversations we had on the phone brought life to me, and I learned a lot from their ideas and struggles. Even better, over time, we became friends and confidants. Reaching out with compassion, even if it is just an understanding look or response at the grocery store, can make all the difference.

● ● ● ● ● ● ● ●

Is there another parent or family that could use your compassion right now? What is one thing you could do to ease their burden?

Karma can help

Sometimes as a parent of a child with special needs, it can feel like you give everything you have to this child, and nothing comes back. No gratitude from them. Not even a nod of approval. Nada. As that child grows it is really easy to feel resentment as you are taken for granted. You might sacrifice your favorite activities, and your closest relationships may suffer, but you do not get any credit from your child.

Karma can help.

Karma is an Eastern concept rooted in the concept of balance. There is the promise that if you do something good and kind, it will come back to you. That is the nature of the universe. But here is the thing about Karma. The good you do might come back in an entirely unexpected way and may seem wholly unconnected.

The beauty of Karma is that it frees us from the expectation of a particular response from the people we love and help. They might someday acknowledge our efforts, or they might not. It does not matter, because we know that somewhere else in our lives the good will come back to us. Karma is a wonderful resentment killer.

• • • • • • • • •

What do you secretly wish your child or partner would say to make up for all the extra work you do? What would it mean to let go of these expectations? How would it free up some of your energy?

Grief can do crazy things to you, so forgive yourself for feeling angry or sad

The picture I had in my mind was from one of those vacation full-page spreads in a magazine. The kids were four and three years old, and we were going to the beach. I was so excited about an paradisal time with my children running around and building castles in the sand. I drove my kids out to the Oregon beach with enthusiasm, humming zip-a-dee-doo-da under my breath.

When we got to the beach and my son stepped onto the sand, he started screaming, "Up, Up!" He was having a sensory reaction to the sand and did not want to touch it. It would take a year of therapy to get him to place his bare feet in sand.

Meanwhile, my daughter started to throw sand and generally upset other children playing nearby. We left after fifteen minutes. I felt so disappointed and angry that I wanted to just melt into the wheel of our minivan as we got back on the road for the long trip home. My blissful picture had been washed away like my imagined sandcastles in the surf.

I did not realize that I was starting to grieve. I was grieving for a normal family experience. For years I had visited the beach and seen families enjoying one another in seemingly effortless bliss. I remembered my own experiences as a child finding shells and playing frisbee with my father. These simple and normal things suddenly felt out of reach. As I pondered during the drive home, I realized that my children would not have the same ease of childhood that I had. I grieved for them, and I also grieved that Joy and I had stepped into a family experience that was draining, confusing, and just plain hard.

One of the key teachings during my interfaith chaplaincy training is that grief is messy. When a person has lost a loved one, emotions spill out that you might not expect. The person may begin to deny anything is wrong, or they may suddenly fly into a rage about something small. Elizabeth Kübler-Ross, a well-known expert on grief, theorized that people seemed to respond to grief though five stages: denial, anger, bargaining, depression, and acceptance.

What I have noticed in my work with parents of kids with special needs and/or disabilities is that they also go through the same stages of grief. These stages of grief are not distinct phases or levels, but are more like a multi-flavored ice cream. The experiences melt into one another and can come in different intensities and at different times.

Denial is often where people begin their journey of grief. It might be that the news is just too big to swallow, and so you protect yourself from the worst of it by denying the reality. In this case, it might mean that a teacher asks a parent to have their child tested, and the parent reacts by denying that anything could be wrong.

Another layer of grief is *anger*. Once the reality of the impairment is absorbed, you might feel angry with yourself, your partner, or the world in general. That anger can spill out into your work and relationships. This might be where you believe that you have been wronged by God or the universe, and you are so angry you are ready to burst. It might be you are angry at the person closest to you or at the person who gets your order wrong at the coffee shop. Someone who innocently comments about your children might get the venomous strike of your anger.

Bargaining is that layer of grief where we think we can change the reality of the moment by making a deal. You might say to God or to the universe that you will be a better person if only your child could be spared this pain. You might look for miracle therapies that will give you a "typical" child. Bargaining is a desperate attempt to control a situation. We are like a child trying to catch a rainbow, endlessly hopeful and frustrated. It also can rob us of enjoying the real progress our child is making.

Depression can be at the clinical level where we are not able to function at all in our daily living, or it can be more like static noise, always in the background. When we are depressed, everyday activities like taking our child to school or therapy can feel like a lead weight. You know what you should do, but you don't have the energy to make anything happen. When we are depressed, we can lose hope, and joy is almost impossible to find.

Acceptance is that layer where we have processed our grief and we accept our new reality. This is the pathway to enjoying your child. It is not in fixing yourself, your parenting, or even your child. Enjoying your child is found in letting go of control and accepting that your life has changed. Once you have accepted your child's special needs, you can begin to rebuild your world. Your relationships will change, and you might even find yourself a more stable and secure person than before you had your exceptional child.

I personally spent a lot of time as a parent in *denial, bargaining,* and *depression.* I kept thinking that I could give my children enough therapies to make their needs go away. The reality was that they were improving but still far behind their typical peers. When we are depressed, it is hard to function, and the whole family unit is affected. When I finally accepted that their disabilities would not go away, and that I would always have to help them, even into their adulthood, I felt a sense of peace. Without knowing it, I was journeying toward *acceptance*.

If you are really struggling with parenting right now, you are likely grieving your child's special needs. Give yourself some grace if you feel like you are screwing up, losing your cool, or just struggling to find a smile. You can work through this, but you may need help.

• • • • • • • •

What layers of grief can you acknowledge? Do you have a friend who gets how hard this is? How can you journal about it? Is there a therapist or spiritual leader you trust who can help you move toward acceptance?

Grief can also do crazy things to your spouse or partner

The stages of grief also apply to our partners and spouses. I have a friend whose husband is in denial about their son's special needs. He believes that there is nothing wrong and that his son is just high spirited. (This is a child I have watched literally bounce off the walls while waiting for the school doors to open at the beginning of the day.) In the midst of his denial, he has pulled back from supporting any therapies or behavioral interventions. He is not only *not* helping with the work but also sabotaging the efforts of his wife. While she is working to learn and grow, his denial, even in the face of expert opinion, feels like a direct undermining of her efforts. It is no wonder that their marriage is precarious at best. How can he not see what is so obvious to others?

The answer is likely that he is grieving his expectations of family life. The mother, meanwhile, is struggling with her own grief, battling to keep herself out of depression. When both people are grieving without acknowledging that grief with each other, the result can be catastrophic. No wonder we parents of kids with special needs are two times more likely to end up divorced. If you have a marriage that is held together by a fraying string, what can you do to acknowledge grief together? Even if the marriage is beyond repair or is over, acknowledging the loss could make the separation and healing gentler.

• • • • • • • • •

Is your partner or other support experiencing some layer of grief? If they are in denial, can you make the invitation to talk about what you feel might be going on?

Grief can also do crazy things to your child

When we first moved to Portland, I met a parent and her daughter at the salon where I had my daughter's hair braided. The girls were about a year apart in age, so I asked if they would be open to a playdate. The mother agreed, and we met at the park. All of a sudden, my son started screaming, and I had to attend to him. Meanwhile, my daughter had a sudden urge to hug her new friend really hard. The other girl started screaming. I ran back to intervene, but the damage was already done. The other girl wanted to go home immediately. My daughter cried herself to sleep that night. She was grieving her loss of a friend, realizing that the world did not line up with her way of being.

Sometimes, I get so frustrated with my daughter and her inability to get dressed and get into the car. My angst can quickly turn to anger when her frustration level starts to rise. Yet every once in a while, I remind myself that she is grieving her loss at some level. All the feelings of grief are her right to express so that she can find her own way to acceptance every day. The funny thing about grief is that when it is given permission to be, joy is almost always around the corner. Joy is not the opposite of grief. Joy is what naturally follows when grief is given its due. When my daughter screams in frustration, I can put my arm around her and say, "Wow, this is really hard for you." I am amazed at how many times she turns and breaks into a sudden smile.

• • • • • • • •

What can you do to acknowledge your child's right to grieve? They might not have the language of grief, but they have the same feelings.

Grief can also do crazy things to the grandparents, and that's OK

My wife and I are lucky that our children's grandparents are understanding and love our children for who they are. Yet, the reality is that most grandparents, especially first-time grandparents, have an image of what grandparenting will be like. They may dream of leisurely walks at the zoo ending with a double-scoop ice cream cone. An aggressive child requiring a special diet is not part of the image.

Grandparents want to bestow their parenting wisdom and can be frustrated when that wisdom does not seem to apply. Perhaps you are the grandparent who has stepped into a parenting role and are dealing with your own grief. Or perhaps you have a parent who has stepped back. Is there some space for you to acknowledge their grief? If seeing people as grieving helps with your anger toward your relatives, please use that image. If you don't have the energy or space for that, focus on your own grief and let go of some of your expectations for a while.

• • • • • • • •

What expectations are you willing to name? Which ones can you let go?

Grief when you are doing this alone

I have a good friend who is divorced and trying to help her adolescent child with special needs while returning to work full time. All people going through divorce are working through grief for the relationship, but when a separation occurs and there's a child with special needs, this grief doubles. The fatigue alone can be enough to cause depression and a sense of impossibility.

The reality is that people often find their best selves in these circumstances. They might not see it, but the single parents I have met are some of the best people humanity has to offer. How do they do it? How do people find the courage to take to this task alone?

Some can't do it. Some people going through any kind of grief (whether they are alone or not) turn to substances like drugs or alcohol to numb out the pain and expectations. But people who are able to acknowledge their feelings in small doses and stay organized may find themselves growing into a new kind of strength. If you are alone, find your community and take it one thing at a time.

You will have to be organized and dig deeper. But single parents can manage very well. They are also some of the most amazing, strongest people one will ever meet.

● ● ● ● ● ● ● ● ●

If you are alone, where can you find sources of courage? Is there a poem or a piece of music that always inspires courage in you? If you are tired, how can you tap into people in your community that might give you respite? What is one part of your daily routine that could use some organization, like a having a place for the kids' shoes or a hook for your car keys?

Everything is harder at night, so prepare during the day

During the day, many of us with kids with special needs are used to being prepared. We carry extra diapers and changes of clothes. If the kid is older, we keep records of homework or doctor visits. We know that anything could happen. We are prepared physically.

What we are not always prepared for are the random wakeup calls during the night. We are up (as I was the other night), and, swaying like a zombie, we walk to the distressed child. All the filters that run during the day are as blurred as our vision woken. We come to the aid of our child who is emotionally disregulated and angry about being awake. Stress levels go up, and suddenly we are in a power struggle with our child, as words we would never utter during the day pass effortlessly through our lips. The whole encounter is like a wreck in slow motion.

What if we could also prepare for moments like these? What if, during the day, we planned what we will do if we get woken up at night by an angry child?

When I was on call during chaplaincy training, I had to be ready to go into very intense situations within minutes of being woken up. In order to be ready, I had my clothes laid out, my scriptures ready, and a centering word or prayer for myself as I went out the door. I remember one night, I walked into a room where a family had just lost their child, and their anger was focused on the first safe person who walked through the door: me!

If you are striving to be more mindful in your parenting, what are the moments when you are the most emotionally vulnerable? Is it before dinner? Is it in the middle of the night? Take time right now to consider what your plan will be if you are needed at that weakest time. Is there a word that you can put on a sticky note in the hallway, like "peace," or a funny word that makes you smile, like "gongoozle" (meaning to gawk at something in an odd way)? Can you create a mind picture or keep an object by the door that can hold your calm for you while you are waking up?

Prepare during the day for an interruption in the night, and you might find yourself a little less drained. Going to sleep earlier also never hurts— that is, if they let you go to sleep in the first place

● ● ● ● ● ● ● ●

What are the moments in your day when you're most vulnerable? Bedtime? During the night? The morning? What's one thing you can do to help you prepare for this vulnerable time?

Let them live with less to enjoy their life more

Sometimes after taking a short break and leaving the kids with someone else, we come back to a house totally destroyed. Every toy is out on the floor and all bins have been dumped over. Our daughter is a seeker, meaning she has the impulse to seek new sensations. She loves chaos and the thrill of looking for something. She used to say, "I'm looking for something." We would desperately ask her to tell us what she was looking for, and she would say that she did not know yet! She just liked looking.

At that time, she was our only child, and we lavished her with whatever we could find that could feed her need to explore. I kept looking for the magic toy that would finally occupy her for more than a few minutes. This seems like a universal challenge for all families. I had a friend who bought every new gizmo and gadget for their son. They had toys literally up to the ceiling.

So many parents I have run into have commented how their toys are never played with except when other children come over. Kids love other children's toys but seem bored with their own. Yet, many of us hoard more and more toys and stuffed animals for our children. We are buried in all the stuff.

One day it occurred to me that one of the pillars of Islam might give us a surprising way out. Islam has a holy time called Ramadan. This is the time, once a year, where people fast, abstaining from food, water, and other comforts, from sunup to sundown. At night people often feast and enjoy time together. I have heard from my Islamic friends that food tastes better during Ramadan and that their joy actually increases as they live more simply.

Recently, I started to apply the basics of fasting, found in almost all major faiths, to everyday home life. For the kids this meant that I made a separate storage area for some of their favorite toys. I started to require that they "fast" from some toys and completely give away others. We kept some puzzles out, along with the basics for imaginary play, but everything else was put away for a time. Later, when I bring out the toys, the kids enjoy a birthday-like influx of toys. The toys are savored because they seem new. With fewer toys, cleanup is faster, and there's more room to dance and play.

Amazingly, fasting from the "stuff" made room for enjoying simple things. Ramadan is a practice that can be a surprise boon for all of us.

• • • • • • • •

What can you do to organize a "fast" from certain toys? What toys are never used and could simply be removed?

Live with less to enjoy your life more

Problems are rarely solved by buying more stuff. Inevitably, the answer is almost always found in simple, everyday things. For example, at one point we owned four strollers for one kid! A baby sitter asked why we had so many strollers. I gave her a long-winded explanation: one didn't work because my wife needed to pull our child, and if she missed the curb it would fall over. We kept trying new ones. Finally we found one that worked, but then we bought a new car, and the perfect one wouldn't fit inside.

I think we bought the strollers so that we could look "normal" as we walked around town. It was what we saw most other people doing. We kept trying to fix the problem with more versions of the normalcy we were craving, and it just did not work.

Ironically, my wife decided to carry our daughter on her back in a carrier. The carrier was a fraction of the cost and allowed my spouse to have both hands free to use her guide dog. The simplest solution had arisen naturally. When we let go of our image of what we thought things should look like, we were able to find the obvious solution. The stroller lesson was an expensive one, but has since helped us to keep the credit card in check.

The same thing can happen with juggling special needs with the kiddos. The new electronic gizmo, or the product catalog that promises to fix all your child's limitations, can leave you with a closet full of half-tries and plastic whatcha-ma-call-its that stress you out and drain your hope just to look at them. Think simple, live with less, and see what adaptations come naturally. The less you have, the more you are free to think on your feet. You might just find yourself with more money in your wallet, and a better solution to boot.

• • • • • • • • •

Before you order that next fix-it solution, can you convince yourself to wait a week or two? What can you accomplish with the items already in your home? What have you done with all those adaptive items you never used? Can you donate them to a local charity that works with children with special needs?

Regression hurts, but learn to embrace it

The other day my daughter decided to play Russian roulette with her life. After a therapy appointment, she was so revved up that she ran out of the building and bolted down the sidewalk. *She will stop at the corner. She will be OK,* I thought.

I kept my inner voice on calm, but then I panicked as I saw that she was not going to stop. She ran across the street!

"Stay over there! I'll meet you over there!"

She bolted back, this time with her eyes closed.

Then she did it again.

Did I mention she is faster than any five-year-old has the right to be? Later that night, I grieved. I had thought the bolting was over, and finally I could get off my toes and relax whenever we transitioned. Running across the street was a phase I thought we had worked through, yet here was the defiant death run back in its full glory. I shared the incident with a friend, who reminded me that regression happens. In fact, regression is part of the journey toward something better.

Regression rips holes in the platitude, "This too shall pass." For parents with kids with special needs, this will pass again and again.

The funny thing is, when we make peace with the fact that regression happens, and might even be necessary for growth, we can stop the stressful yo-yo of thinking that our child is or is not progressing. If your child is playing a version of Russian roulette, don't let them trigger you. This too shall pass … and pass again.

• • • • • • • •

Has your child ever taken 2 steps forward, only to take 3 steps back? Think back to a time when that happened, then recognize where your child is now. Does it give you any relief?

We regress, too, and that too is how we grow.

The other day, I really stepped in it. I had a migraine and had broken my own rule of no TV at night, so I was exhausted. My daughter's teacher made a comment about our always being late, and I snapped back. Upsetting the people who have your back with your kids is not the way you want to start your day.

Later that day, I was waiting for my daughter and forgot to turn off my car engine. Another parent, who was also having a bad day, came out of the school and told me to turn off my car. I received a lecture on how my fumes were making it harder for the kids with special needs. I am pretty sure he thought I was just an obnoxious stranger. I could have retorted that I had not one, but two kids in the "special" school. But this time, I did not snap back. I had recognized from the morning that I was having a bad parenting day, and this parent's probably wasn't sunshine and roses, either. Besides, I was in the wrong, so I just said, "OK," and turned off my car. Sometimes just knowing that we are all stressed out, makes things, well. . . less stressful.

As parents, we regress, too. We may be full of mindfulness for a while, but then we slide back into old habits. Take it easy on yourself if you are mindful and grounded for a while and then suddenly lose it. Your kids will not implode, and you are not a terrible person. This is just part of being human and vulnerable to the same temptations as our kids. I find my best parenting moments are when I really blow it and am able to share my process of accepting my faults and keeping up my self-image.

What are the times when you have regressed lately? How can you let it go and begin to model grace for your kids?

Put wonder in their day through waiting

My daughter does not like getting into her bath. I have a pile of sticker charts soaked with the tears of us both that chronicle the bath wars saga. After trying everything and then some, I finally gave up attempting to fix the problem in traditional ways. I decided to embrace my daughter's innate curiosity and sense of wonder. I told her that I was writing her a special note, and in the morning when she got into the bath, it would be waiting for her. She loved this new game.

This is similar to what the Christian church does when it helps people prepare for Christmas with the season of Advent, a waiting time. Waiting for something, just like waiting for a child to be born, puts wonder into everyday things. For an older child, the wonder might be a new privilege that can only be revealed when they reach a goal. Or maybe it is putting a family vacation plan in an envelope that will be ceremonially revealed when the house is all cleaned up together.

Waiting puts wonder into your child and lightens your burden as a parent, because their anticipation is the best gift a parent could get. It is hope in its purest form, and that hope is what will give you the resilience to get through the challenge, even if you both end up soaked in the reality of how hard this work is.

• • • • • • • •

What are some Advent moments you can invent to inspire wonder in you and your child?

Take a break, because your resilience is more important than their progress

We have all been to the dark side of the moon, where we can't seem to scrounge up any more energy or determination. It may be hard to get out of bed and far too easy to crawl into it. For me, it is those times when nothing seems to be helping or working to get my child to the next developmental stage. The feeling of helplessness is like carbon monoxide for your soul.

This is the time when it is important to focus on yourself for a while, and less on your child's progress. You might even need a vacation from therapies. I remember a time last year when I had eight therapy appointments in one week. It was too much. I was transporting kids four hours a day, and I was not able to cook or clean; we were living in filth and eating fast food. We needed a break.

We took a break from all therapies for two weeks. I started exercising again and caught up on laundry. I took better care of myself, and my energy came back. During that break, we had some very difficult challenges that would probably have broken my spirit if they had happened when I was spread too thin. Thank goodness we had strengthened our resilience with some rest.

• • • • • • • •

If you are going through some challenges, how can you give yourself permission to take a break? Do you have a relationship that needs to heal? Do you need to give your back a break? Taking care of yourself will keep up your resiliency, and that is more important than making it to every therapy. After all, loving your child to the moon and back means giving your soul a chance to recharge its engines.

It's not a haircut, so why are people so nosy?

Recently, I noticed a woman with haircut similar to my wife's. I told Joy about the haircut, and she immediately asked the woman where she got it cut and the name of the stylist. This was harmless curiosity with a little bit of purpose attached. We had a pleasant conversation with the stranger, and then we all went on with our lives.

Sometimes people's curiosity can be a little less harmless. Have you ever met someone who seems uncomfortably curious about your kid's special needs? They might ask you straight up what their diagnoses are, personal questions about their histories. Depending on how your kids entered your family, they might ask if they were exposed to drugs in utero. They might ask if you had problems with your pregnancy. Such personal questions! Why are people so nosy? Don't they know that people may have significant trauma around these questions?

The answer is no. People don't know that such questions feel invasive and personal. To them it is like a haircut, something to talk about. They might think it's small talk, chit-chat, though they might be asking you about things that you have not yet told your family or your best friend. How do you deal with this invasion?

There have been times when I did not feel prepared for invasive questions. I felt defensive, not ready to deal with the conversation.

Then I learned from a friend with a disability a magic phrase that works most of the time. I say, "Why do you ask?"

Sometimes this backfires, and the person gets angry or defensive, but most of the time, people will share a personal story or connection and move on. If all else fails, as another good friend, whose child has a disability, reassured me, I never owe anyone information about my child, even my family or friends. Give yourself permission to draw your lines of privacy and choose for yourself when you are ready to cross them.

• • • • • • • •

What are some phrases you can have on hand in case someone asks a question you're not ready to answer?

Carry something small to remind you of something big

Michael had a worn-out stuffed animal that he used to carry everywhere all the time. It was a disgusting little thing that I wished would leave us magically like the Velveteen Rabbit. His animal of choice was a tiger whose stripes were so worn that it looked more like a mouse—a chewed-up mouse not long for this world. As much as I wanted him to lose the tiger, I also understood that his tiger was the only object he still had from infancy. It was something small that reminded him of a bigger sense of security.

As adults we could learn a thing or two from our children. We too need something small to remind us of something bigger than ourselves. I have a number of Sikh friends who travel with a sword at all times. The Kirpan, as it is called, is more than a weapon, it is a symbol. It can be three feet long or thee centimeters; the size does not matter. The Kirpan reminds the wearer of a courage and obligation that is bigger than themselves. They are reminded that it is their duty to step up and defend their community at any time.

What would be a good Kirpan for you? Is there a poem or a photo that you keep on your phone? Is there a voice mail that you never delete because it gives you strength? Your Kirpan could be a charm bracelet or a ring with your children's birthstones. I have a good friend who tattooed her children's initials on her body. Right now, I keep a pink ribbon in my car to remind me to be strong as we have two parents with cancer. I sometimes offer a prayer at a stoplight when I see the ribbon hanging in our minivan. My wife has pictures of our children that I keep updated at her desk at work. Someone asked why she had them, since she cannot see them. She said simply, "I know that they are there."

The next time you have to confront a stranger who does not understand your kids, or when you are on the phone with your insurance company, carry something small that reminds you of your strength and courage. Your Kirpan, your birth ring, or your tattoo may be just what you need to keep your inner tiger intact.

● ● ● ● ● ● ● ●

Do you have a birthday or special occasion coming up, and people want gift ideas? Consider asking for something small and symbolic that will give you strength. Do you already have something? A picture? A baby shoe? Can you put it in your pocket or purse?

Pain is often paired with shame. Deal with both.

Even among other parents who have a child with special needs, there is a secret pain we don't easily share. We may feel comfortable talking about our struggles and the difficulties of parenting. We may even compare bruises and broken noses (my wife and I have received both from our kids!) But it is hard to talk about the shame beneath the pain and disappointment. Shame is like a silent lurking monster under the bed that we cannot see, but is silently present and in a very real way changes our sense of security in the world.

In Korean there is word that is hard to translate into Western thought. It is a concept called *han*. The closest word we have may be shame. Yet *han* is more than shame. It is the idea that when we are wounded there is a feeling of dishonor that is just as harmful to us as the wound itself. The victim must find healing for both to become whole again.

I know that I feel an intense shame when my kids act out in public. I remember I was giving the message at a church service when I was quietly informed that three adults were working together to try to calm down my children in the nursery. Three adults could not control them, and the caregivers needed help fast! Behind the pain of not being normal as a family, there's a sense that somehow we should still be able to "fix" our kids. The children's shortcomings can feel like a dishonor.

• • • • • • • •

The first step in dealing with your han is to acknowledge those feelings of shame in a healthy way. Can you journal or talk to a close friend? Is there a faith community or meditation center that can help you find healing? What about a family therapist? Even though you are the parent, you have been wounded at times by your child, and it is good to process that toward your own healing.

Han happens for our kids, too

Our children also have *han*. Perhaps your child's disability was the result of a chemical exposure or an accident of some kind. Perhaps their wounds are from their growing self-awareness that they are different. They may even have a sense of shame caused by how we as parents have reacted to them.

The other day, I called out my daughter's social mistake of hugging a child too hard. In the past, she would take my instruction and move on. Now she was embarrassed that she had made a mistake, and she experienced *han* in that moment. Her *han* so disregulated her that she took off down the street like she had just seen Godzilla. No, it was as if she *were* Godzilla, scaring all the people unlucky enough to be in her path.

As my kids grow older, I am more aware of their *han* and that their woundedness goes deeper than I sometimes realize.

• • • • • • • •

How can you be more mindful of these feelings your child has deep down? How can you reflect these feelings back for them so they can find healing for the shame? Just knowing about your kid's han may give you a deeper empathy and may tame the monster called shame.

An ounce of silly is worth a pound of serious

It is counter-intuitive, but big doses of seriousness can actually undermine our authority, while being silly may elicit surprising responses from our child.

Think about it. When our leaders use humor, we lean toward them with admiration, whether or not we agree with them philosophically. I remember Ronald Reagan pretending with a chuckle that the microphones were broken when he was asked about the Iran-Contra affair. Everyone laughed. It is those unexpected comedic moments during a tense interchange that endear people to us. It is not their rants or their philosophical speeches. We may disagree with them, but their good humor eases the aggitation, so we're more apt to listen.

The same is true with our kiddos. When we dig in with our expectations and hold the hard line, we may be helping our kiddos to practice breaking though our authority. Silliness may actually teach them how to take life less seriously and how to manage their own frustration.

The other day, my son was at a music class when he went into a tirade about not wanting to comply with the music therapist's instructions. "No, no, no!" he shouted.

Normally, I would get very serious and counter his obnoxiousness with some "good discipline." Instead, I said, "Blow, blow, blow!" and "Grow, grow, grow!" Then I pretended my nose was running.

He stopped in his tantrum as I continued tickling his right brain with silly goofiness. He slowly settled out of his Amygdala, that part of the brain responsible for fight or flight modality, and he joined me in being goofy. He then immediately complied with the teacher. Later the teacher emailed me how much she had learned from the experience. Silliness was a new tool for her!

Silliness also helps me get out of my left-brained stubbornness. I feel less tired at the end of the day. It turns out that being silly is the secret weapon of the happy parent of kids with special needs. Life is simply too short to miss out on silliness.

• • • • • • • •

How can you be sillier so that you can gain emotional authority with your child?

Practice counts more when you are exhausted

I have a good friend who puts me to shame with his discipline. He is a stay-at-home dad of two kids and a part-time engineer. He also finds time to produce animated movies in his basement. He drove his station wagon across the country ... with his two-year-old. Need I say more?

I asked him one day about his discipline and how he is able to sustain himself. He shared that he had once been a gymnast and had even been an Olympic hopeful for the pommel horse. The thing about gymnastics, he said, is that on a good day, your routine is a piece of cake. Anybody can win a competition on a good day, when your body feels good and you are ready to engage. The trick was to be able to do a better than average routine on days when your body felt out of sorts and horrible. The only way to do that, he shared, was to practice your routine even on your really off days. Practicing through the awkward days made it possible to compete no matter how your body felt.

Being a parent is such a physical and mental activity. The daily routines are hard to keep up, and some days it is easier to leave the messes and not work ahead for the next day. There are times that I do just that.

However, I began to see my friend's discipline as a good reminder, that parenting is a discipline, an Olympic event every day. When I practiced/faked mindfulness on the migraine, up-all-night, spacey days, I was training my body and soul to be mindful and perform moderately well all the time. When I was exhausted, I started to think about training myself and how this was when the practice really counted.

• • • • • • • • •

Rather than giving up on hard days, how can you add value to them by continuing your routines? What can you do that will train your body to respond with love and care when your kids need you? This does not mean that you try harder, or beat yourself up to be more disciplined. It just means that you commit to making consistent, doable choices over time. You are an Olympian, so get back on that pommel horse, and train with some discipline, especially on the hard days.

Someone always has it harder than you

Sometimes I get overwhelmed and feel sorry for myself. It seems to happen most often over small things, like when Nicole refuses to get in the car because she wants the stimulation of creating conflict, or Michael screams because his socks are on inside out. I sometimes get frustrated that my blind and (at the time of this writing) pregnant wife is not able to help me as much as others' spouses do, by giving the kids a bath or driving them to appointments.

One particularly difficult morning, after listening to a friend, I realized that my morning was really not that hard after all. My good friend told me that her son was smearing his poop all over the walls and floor at home. This is a lot more common than people know. I had a moment to realize that on particularly crappy days, someone, somewhere, always has it crappier. We don't always have that perspective.

• • • • • • • •

Do you feel sorry for yourself today? I guarantee someone has it worse. Have you jumped online lately and read other people's stories? Do you have a support group in your area? Can you have a phone date with a friend going through the same things? If you take five minutes to do this, you can free yourself from feeling you have it worst.

This is not a competition

I remember sharing with a friend about this book, and she immediately told me about a book written by a woman with not just two, but three kids with special needs. This writer did not even have a partner. She was on her own.

I immediately felt an odd sense of inadequacy, since my life was obviously easier than hers. Maybe I did not have any right to add to the conversation. Maybe one's life had to be a lot harder to be of interest to anyone else. It is easy to get into a feeling of competition to see who has it worst when sharing with other people with exceptional kids. When our identity gets confused with our work with our own kiddos, we can feel inadequate upon meeting someone who has it harder.

What would happen if we stopped being impressed by how hard people had it, and focused more on what we could do for each other? We all have something important to share.

I spent some time attending Quaker services with a small group in the hills of Southern Oregon. Quakers believe that everyone has a piece of the Divine Wisdom and should be allowed to share it if they felt the Spirit move them. In this fellowship, I was particularly moved when a child would share, or a person with a developmental disability would teach us. It was a stunning reminder that wisdom can be played on any instrument.

It does not matter if your life is easy or hard, or who has it hardest. We all have a piece of divine wisdom and can lean on each other. You have nothing to prove, and your situation warrants any degree of complaining or wisdom gleaning that comes to you.

How can you give yourself permission to be wise?

• • • • • • • •

What can you do to minimize competition with your friends and become more of a support on their journeys?

Lean on your culture, but don't let your background push you where you don't want to go

You may have an easily identified culture of origin, or you may consider yourself as not having any specific culture at all. No matter who you are, you have a culture, and it does affect you. Whether you are a native of your country or an immigrant, the structure of who you are is supported by the pillars of the culture that bear you up. This is never more obvious than when you marry or partner with someone of a different background or heritage. Even if you are single, you may not have considered how your own culture drives you.

I was brought up in an Indian household, with very specific expectations concerning parenting and home life. In my home, men led the household and made the big decisions. I was not expected to cook or clean, but to bring a steady wage into the home. Also, in India, disability is considered a weakness and something that carries shame.

Part of my journey was to recognize those cultural values and pick and choose what would help me. I had to reject my cultural expectations of being a man. I put on my apron and did most of the cleaning. I did all the potty training and meal preparations. I also rejected the idea that a person with a disability had less to offer society. At the same time, some parts of my home culture were helpful: respecting all elders, taking great care of books, giving time to your family, taking care of your parents. These were parts of my culture that I did not want to lose.

I also loved that my wife's Dutch culture supported frugality and hard, honest work. When my partner and I could step back and be mindful of our different family cultures, we could mix and match in ways that strengthened our family unit. When we don't recognize that we are speaking from our cultures, we can descend into bickering and frustration.

• • • • • • • •

What is your culture? With what values did you grow up? What can you let fall away? What are the value pillars that will hold up your family today?

Your child needs to see you thrive and enjoy life

It is easy to be the savior, the martyr, the one who gives it all to make your family thrive.

I remember the difficult decision to leave my dream job and take time to be home to support my daughter. It was the right choice for her, and for me as well. Stepping back is a valid choice for a lot of people, and it is often a courageous choice.

At the same time, don't abandon every aspect of your previous life. One day my daughter was surprised that I knew about something about a church. That seemed strange, since I had been working in churches for nearly two decades. It occurred to me that she thought that all I could do was take care of her. Why wouldn't she think that? That was all she could remember me doing.

It suddenly occurred to me that I was modeling sacrifice for her, but I was not modeling how to live a fulfilled life. Somehow all the things that gave me joy, like running, playing music, or leading church services, had slowly been scratched off my calendar. My daughter could not see me as someone who had mastered anything, because all she had seen me do was parent.

If we are to teach our children to have fulfilled lives and interests, they have to see us doing other things as well.

• • • • • • • •

What is one interest that fulfills you? How can you downsize it so that it is doable right now in your calendar? How can you bring back something from it to celebrate it in your home life? Is it pottery or other visual art you can put on the counter? Is it a tennis racket that you can hang up in a prominent place, or are there pictures of you having fun with your new friends? Living your life with joy and sharing out of that joy is one of the greatest gifts we can give our children.

Stormy kids make the best rainbows

Nicole has a rainbow-making machine that her grandmother sent her in the mail. It is a simple little toy that casts a large rainbow over the entire room. Grandma sent it because our daughter was having night terrors and the rainbow was something Nicole could turn on when she was scared.

Rainbows mean a lot to me, not just because I live in rainy Portland. Rainbows mean a lot because, as a parent of kids with special needs, I need hope to win out over despair.

In Judeo-Christian stories, the rainbow appeared to a world that had been completely decimated. Everything had to start from scratch. The rainbow came as a promise that such destruction would not happen again (Genesis 9:15-16). It meant that the survivors could rebuild their lives with the assurance that it was safe to begin anew.

If your whole life feels like a flood has wiped out your grounding, rainbows are also for you. Maybe you are going through a divorce, losing your home, or just feel really isolated. You may feel like a boat at sea with no land in sight. Your exceptional child may be at the center of it all or even a part of the problem that started the whole mess.

On the other hand, your child may be what you need to get through it. I have a friend going through a divorce, who said his concern for his child with special needs helped him manage his own way through the pain. Keeping up his child's hope helped him maintain his own.

When I talk about rainbows, I am not saying, "This too shall pass." Too many times people say this but do not recognize the real and permanent destruction in a person's life. When I say that rainbows are for you, I mean that especially in the destructive times of life, everyone needs to create space for hope. Being a resilient parent is acknowledging your losses and being willing to rebuild after each storm.

The message of the rainbow is that every storm has its time, but then it loses its power. If everything has been wiped out in your life, or if that happens in your future, take heart that after the flood, when the time is right, you will rebuild. When light hits a storm at the right angle, the light breaks up into a stunning array of colors. These colors aren't just fancy. They serve as a testimony that when pain is given space and time, it becomes fragmented, no longer a threat, but a witness to better things to come. Keep your hope. If you are drifting, don't panic and force answers. You will land on something solid, and you will rebuild when the time is right.

• • • • • • • • •

What needs rebuilding in your life, and what is giving you hope to begin again? When you think of your life, your narrative, your personal 90-second elevator speech, what are ways that you can invite hope into your story?